Rethinking Gender

Masculinity, Femininity and Queerity in Postcolonial Indian Fiction

Sunita Sinha

ATLANTIC

PUBLISHERS & DISTRIBUTORS (P) LTD

Published by
ATLANTIC
PUBLISHERS & DISTRIBUTORS (P) LTD
7/22, Ansari Road, Darya Ganj, New Delhi-110002
Phones : +91-11-40775252, 23273880, 23275880, 23280451
Fax : +91-11-23285873
Web : www.atlanticbooks.com
E-mail : orders@atlanticbooks.com

Branch Office
5, Nallathambi Street, Wallajah Road, Chennai-600002
Phones : +91-44-64611085, 32413319
E-mail : chennai@atlanticbooks.com

Printed in India at Nice Printing Press, A-33/3A, Site-IV, Industrial Area, Sahibabad, Ghaziabad, U.P.

Preface

> "'Gender' is now one of the busiest, most restless terms in the English language, a word that crops up everywhere, yet whose uses seem to be forever changing, always on the move, producing new and often surprising inflections of meaning."
>
> —*Genders,* David Grover and Cora Kaplan

Since Simone de Beauvoir first proclaimed that "One is not born a woman, one becomes one", the study of gender has become one of the most significant new disciplines in the humanities and social sciences, commanding a relevance that crosses disciplinary boundaries and provokes lively debates. Writing this book was an opportunity to bring together recent works on the articulation of gender in postcolonial Indian Fiction. Recognising the global dimensions of gender change, the book addresses central questions about the analysis and construction of gender in contemporary society. Why are we so persistent that man and woman are unalike? Why does society cleave people into masculine men and feminine women? Why does it see women and men not just as biological organisms but as people shaped by their everyday social world? In this anthology, I have attempted to identify the tensions created by changing sexual roles and expectations as well as point to the way in which they are expressed in the Indian English literature and society. By focusing on the way in which characters are being projected on the literary canvass by Indian writers, I intend to examine the central concerns that affect and influence the feminist, masculinist, and the queer narratives.

Gender is often thought of as a binary identity—male or female—with stereotypical traits and behaviours still attached to each. "*Rethinking Gender: Masculinity, Femininity and Queerity in Postcolonial Indian Fiction*", will attempt in addition to exploring Masculinity and , to look beyond the binary identity, exploring more broad and inclusive conceptualisations of gender expression. Discourses of Masculinity and Femininity have been extensively explored in postcolonial narratives. However, gendered representations in fiction also embraces the new emergent stream of Queer literature, which has been given visibility in the public consciousness through compelling stories and canvasses. Hence, the book aims at providing a comprehensive analysis of the key debates informing the dynamics of women's studies—focusing on women, femininity and the relationships between power and gender; men's studies—with a focus on men or masculinity, feminism, gender, and politics; queer studies—concerned with orientation issues related to sexual cross-gender identities. "*Rethinking Gender: Masculinity, Femininity and Queerity in Postcolonial Indian Fiction*" is a humble effort to bring together all these aspects of gender studies beautifully manifested in some of the significant works by eminent novelists in postcolonial Indian English literature.

Since the last couple of decades of the last century, the topic of Masculinity has attracted much critical and scholarly light. Academic work on masculinity has developed across a number of disciplines including literature, cultural studies, and sociology as well as film and media studies, and has often evolved in dialogue with feminist politics, sharing concerns regarding the ideologies of gender discourses and critiquing the power relations that are at play in a patriarchal society.

With the onset of Renaissance in England, MAN suddenly came into focus. The glorification of manhood received a fillip when the British naval forces under Sir Francis Drake defeated the so-called invincible Spanish Armada in 1588. The Augustan age ushered in the concept of homo economicus—men, and not women, were at the fountain head of trade and commerce —and the Rousseauvean concept of the Noble Savage was an exaltation of masculinity. Baden Powell's Scout Movement and numerous travelogues reflect the pride of the colonial masters in masculinity. The political and theoretical challenges issued by contemporary feminism have provoked a range of cultural responses about men and about masculinity. Masculinity is a way to explain and describe the broad spectrum of realities associated with men and their worldview—but there are different ideas captured with different terminology: biological determinism or essentialism, the normative definition, which says masculinity is what, ought to be, cultural or social constructionism as well as masculinity as a power discourse. In the view of biological determinists, masculinity is men's basic nature, and as such helps to explain not only differences but also inequalities between men and women. Men's political, economic, and cultural entitlements arise from their being 'masculine', as variously reflected in genetic predisposition to aggression, physical strength, and sexual drives in contrast to passivity, weakness, and sexual reserve of femininity. Normative views stresses on social norms and study of normative stereotypes or 'normative ideals', which a man or woman out to be or do. This view can also be implacable in understanding 'Dharma' or 'Jaati dharma' as reflected in expressions like 'Kshatriya dharma', in classical writings on caste and *varna* system in India.

The first chapter opens with "Understanding Masculinities", which tries to present a panoramic view of masculinity in postcolonial Indian fiction tracing in detail its origin, development, and current relevance in the academia today. It situates questions of masculinity within an interdisciplinary context that connects with cultural studies, sociology, and wider media. Focusing on representations of masculinity in postcolonial Indian fiction, the next two consecutive sections in the first chapter, "Mapping Masculinities in the Fiction of Raja Rao and Representations of Masculinities in Anita Desai's Novels" explore masculinities in the fiction of two acclaimed Indian novelists and comment how postcolonial Indian fiction has engaged with masculinity. Masculinity is essentially a social construct. So, it is inevitable that this book will draw upon sociology. Moreover, concepts from feminist theories will also be used because the feminist theories not only provide a counter discourse to studies on masculinities, the feminist theories also provide a parallel insight into various socially sanctioned roles set up by a patriarchal society. The concept of 'masculinities,' informed by recent feminist thought and the women's movement, has emerged as a means of renewing feminist discourse by encouraging a more relational approach to masculinities and femininities. Thus, Masculinity studies are a significant outgrowth of Feminist studies and an ally to its older sister in a complex and constantly shifting relationship.

There would have been no gender studies without feminism as a driving force. But, whereas gender studies is a field of knowledge and study, feminism is both a political movement and a field of knowledge and study, the latter being called feminist research or feminist theory. The terms gender studies and feminist research are sometimes used synonymously for the discipline. Other researchers in the field distinguish between gender studies and feminist research. Feminism in such cases represents a more critical approach with a perspective on power.

The second chapter, "Framing the Feminine", explores the history, development, types, and various waves of Feminism in the contemporary scenario. Feminism in Indian English novels is a much discussed concept. Over the years many Indian women writers, from Toru Dutt to Kamala Das and from Sarojini Naidu to Suniti Namjoshi, Arundhati Roy to Shashi Deshpande have in their own way, tried to convey their thoughts in a distinct personal voice, and in the process, have brilliantly evolved a collective tone emphasising the sovereignty of women. Breaking the boundaries of routine directions in literary narratives, the women writers, along with the simultaneous assimilation of Pan-Indian elements, have turned their creativity a formidable area of study and research. Further, the two sections of the second chapter, *Perspectives on Femininity and Masculinity in Shashi Deshpande's That Long Silence* and *Crossing Lines and Reappropriating Female Space in Arundhati Roy's The God of Small Things,* discuss at length the feminine mystique and slants in the above mentioned novels.

Queer is originally a derogatory label for homosexuals, but in the context of gender studies it is used in connection with homosexuality research and with efforts to combat the normative status of heterosexuality in society and culture. Queer fiction has brought about a change in the way in which we understand literary and aesthetic expression since the early 1980s. It has involved, for instance, ironic reconstructions of traditional gender roles, reimagining supposedly heterosexual characters in literature as, in fact, closeted gay lovers, and trying to make previously marginal forms of pleasure and desire into perfectly acceptable mainstream ones. Earlier, novels on same-sex relationships were rare in Indian writing in English. However, in the past couple of years, this scenario is undergoing a transformation. With more authors going for homosexual themes for their work, a same-sex story no longer remains a taboo for Indian writers. Queer scholar Ruth Vanita's work on Indian sexualities is both prolific and covers a wide range of queer representations, from historical to the literary and popular culture.

Exploring the historical, cultural, and social position of the queer subject in postcolonial India, the third chapter, "Narrating Queerness", reviews several contemporary queer writings in India and creates a starting point for discussions on India's queer sexuality. Examining texts which focus on queer spatial reclamation from the periphery to the center, and "challenging the heteropatriarchal spatial deployment found in mainstream narratives and dominant cultural practices in India," the concluding section, "Queer Sexualities in R. Raj Rao's *The Boyfriend*", in the third chapter, counters the disempowerment of the queer community in postcolonial India. The transgender, gender-atypical or intersex protagonist challenges normative assumptions and expectations about gender, identity, and sexuality.

Sunita Sinha

Contents

Chapter 1
Understanding Masculinities

MASCULINITIES IN THE GLOBAL CONTEXT

The critical interrogation of men and masculinities is a relatively recent phenomenon emerging out of the second wave feminism of the 1970s and 1980s. Prior to this, history was very much his-story, throughout which men continued to be at the centre. The critical debate woven around the analysis of men is not more than two decades old, but the developments arising from this debate is never the less very profound. There are discussions about multiplicity of masculinities, the significance of social and cultural influences on masculinities, the various aspects of hegemonic masculinity, and changes in dominant male and subordinate ones, emerging from the exploration and understanding of masculinities.

In his introduction to *Changing Men*, the U.S. sociologist of men and masculinities, Michael Kimmel, explains that: "As women's studies have radically revised the traditional academic canon, men's studies seek to use that revision as the basis for its exploration of men and masculinity" (Kimmel 10). Men's studies opens up a space that "attempts to treat masculinity not as the normative referent against which standards are assessed but as a problematic gender construct" (Kimmel 10). Masculinity can be seen as an ideology which developed out of men's fear of extinction due to the patriarchal sexual division of labour by the rise of modernity. All the power, resources and privileges which man earlier enjoyed by the sheer virtue of his sex, had now to be asserted by men due to the socially constructed gender identity which spelt out a certain undefined natural difference. Over the past decade, many researches explore the multiple questions that arise as a result of understanding masculinity as a gender construct. Contemporary men's studies arises from a history of debates about gender relations, men, and masculinities, yet represents a new departure based on social analysis of gender and close-focus empirical work. Thus, we can say that the notions of masculinity depends on several factors, including the historical context, geographic location, class standing, ethnicity, culture, age, marital status, sexuality and various individual differences. Therefore, masculinity is not a stable construct; it is varied in its construction and in its enactment.

Defining Masculinity

Definitions of masculinity, however, are not the expressions of some inner essence, nor do they bubble up through biological composition. The search for a transcendent, timeless definition of manhood is itself a sociological phenomenon—society tends to search for the timeless and eternal during moments of crisis, those points of transition when old definitions no longer work and new definitions are yet to be firmly established. It is important to think of manhood in a different way: as a constantly changing collection of meanings that are constructed through relationships with themselves, with other men, and with the world. A social constructionist perspective understands gender definitions as neither static nor timeless, but historically articulated within and through people's interactions with their worlds. According to Connell, "Masculinity does not exist except in contrast with feminity. A culture which does not treat men and women as bearers of polarized character types, at least in principle, does not have a concept of masculinity in the sense of modern European/ American culture" (Connell 2005: 68). Beasley considers the Masculinity Studies field to be largely pro-feminist and social constructivist in nature (Beasley 2005). Masculinity has been, generally, defined as a way to describe man, manliness, being vigorous, being active, having qualities considered approximate to a true man. Our understanding about masculinity has been redefined as "different ideologies among different culture and social groups" (Leavant and Sandra 1999) and "masculinity as being central to male gender roles linked to beliefs about the essentiality of men adhering to culturally defined standards for male behaviours" (Pleck 1995). A slight deviation from these 'masculine standards' makes him more prone to be violent, physically, psychologically, as well as sexually. The hegemonic nature of masculinity (Connell 1987) places it over various subordinated masculinities as well as over women in a socio-political hierarchy based on power and control.

The rival ideologies of 'masculine' and 'feminine' are, according to Freud, "among the most confused that occurs in science," and have proved to be rather diffusing to be defined. The word 'masculinity' derives from the Middle English *masculin*, from Middle French and from Latin *masculinus* ('male, of masculine gender,' 'male person, male') and *masculus* (male). It can be defined as "behaviours, languages and practices, existing in specific cultural and organizational locations, which are commonly associated with males and thus culturally defined as not feminine" (Whitehead and Barrett 2001: 15-16). Kate Millet in *Sexual Politics* suggests,

> Male supremacy, like other political creeds, does not finally reside in physical strength but in the acceptance of a value system which is not biological. (Millet 1970)

Mick Leach too defines masculinity thus,

> Unlike the biological state of maleness, masculinity is a gender identity constructed socially, historically and politically. It is the cultural interpretation of maleness, learnt through participation in society and its institutions. (Leach 2008)

The Oxford English Dictionary defines masculinities as "having the qualities or physical features that are admired or expected in a man," the other "having the qualities or appearance typical of men." But what exactly is typical of men, and does everyone expect the same of them? Both of the above definitions are normative, asserting what men ought to be. But, "what is normative about a norm hardly anyone meets?" (Connell 1995: 70). What this question implies is rather vague, namely, that masculinity, just as femininity and gender in general, are social constructions. Neither of these categories "exists organically" (Gittings 1996: 4) they are "a way of structuring social practice" (Connell 1995: 75) fabricated by humans. And just as humans are different from one person to the next, so are their cultures and their social conceptions of masculinity. In other words, "there are multiple masculinities. 'Masculinity' is not a coherent object about which a generalising science can be produced" (Connell 1995: 67). Moreover, it is significant to notice at this point, that the different concepts of masculinity are always tightly interwoven with other social constructs and the respective expectations thereof, such as race, gender, class, age, religion, and so forth.

Current masculinity studies are invigorated by a range of feminist, humanist and poststructural theories and current feminist studies are in turn being changed by the insights of masculinity studies. All societies have cultural accounts of gender but not all have the concept 'masculinity'. In its modern usage the term assumes that one's behaviour results from the type of person one is. An unmasculine person can behave differently being peaceable rather violent, conciliatory rather than dominating and so on. Therefore, femininity and masculinity or one's gender identity (Burke, Stets and Pirog-Good 1988; Spence 1985) refers to the degree to which persons see themselves as masculine or feminine given what it means to be a man or woman in society. Femininity and masculinity are rooted in the social (one's gender) rather than the biological (one's sex). Societal members decide what being male or female means (e.g., dominant or passive, brave or emotional), and males will generally respond by defining themselves as masculine while females will generally define themselves as feminine.

Thus, we see that during the last two decades research into men and masculinities has emerged as one of the growth areas of sociological enquiry. With innumerable variations in time and space, masculinity is more complicated than we might first believe and therefore it can be studied not as a single definition, but as variety and complexity. Definitions of masculinity are diverse and ever changing and the ideas of masculinity are far from stable and fixed. No definition of masculinity is completely agreed upon by all. Interestingly, with women acquiring masculinity hormonally and we are left to wondering as to how can masculinity be natural if a woman can become a man? To many of us a French man may appear to be effeminate and Indian students walking hand in hand might appear rather queer and amusing to an American student. A male college professor might appear to be less masculine than a labourer. According to Kimmel, "Men are just beginning to realize that the 'traditional' definition of masculinity leaves them unfulfilled and dissatisfied" (*Gendered* 268).

Socio-Psychological Paradigms

The first steps towards the modern analysis of masculinity are found in the pioneering psychologies of Freud. These demonstrated that adult character was not biologically predetermined but constructed through emotional attachments to others in a turbulent growth process (Connell 1994). Though Freud nowhere wrote a systematic discussion of masculinity, it remained a continuing theme in all his works over thirty years. He provided a method of research, a guiding concept, the dynamic unconscious, and a first map of the development of masculinity. Freud's concept of masculinity was taken up by Alfred Adler, whose argument started from the familiar polarity between masculinity and femininity, but immediately emphasized the feminist point that one side of the polarity is devalued in culture and associated with weakness. Adler considered the masculine protest to be active in normal as well as neurotic mental life. Adler took highly critical view of dominating masculinities, commenting on "the arch evil of our culture, the excessive pre-eminence of manliness". Like Freud, Carl Jung was also concerned with the presence of femininity within men. Jung argued that the feminine interior of masculine men was shaped not only by the life history of the particular man but also inherited 'archetypal' images of women.

> No man is so entirely masculine that he has nothing feminine in him. The fact is rather, that very masculine men have-carefully guarded and hidden—a very soft emotional life, often incorrectly described as 'feminine'.

> A man counts it a virtue to repress his feminine traits as much as possible, just as a woman, at least until recently, considered it unbecoming to be mannish. The repression of feminine traits and inclinations naturally causes these contrasexual demands to accumulate in the unconscious. (Jung 1928/1953: 187)

Anthropologists such as Malinowski and Mead went on to emphasize cultural differences in such processes, structures and norms. By the mid-twentieth century, these ideas had crystallised into the associated concepts of masculinity and the male sex role. The concept of masculinity has also been used in analysing literary and other texts.

Although most enterprises towards gender equality must emphasize women's empowerment, any effort to further gender equality that does not include men is doomed to failure. It was women who made gender visible as a category of analysis, as a variable that must be factored into any discussion of development. Today, although we understand that development is a gendered process, the effect of development on men remains relatively less well-understood. This "invisibility" of masculinity in discussions of development has political dimensions. The invisibility of masculinity reproduces gender inequality, both materially and ideologically. Thus, any initiative to improve the condition of women must include efforts to involve men. The vision of gender equality is impossible without changes in men's lives as well as in women's and it remains our first task is to make masculinity visible in the development process. For this we must analyse the ways in which definitions of masculinity vary. The various social and behavioural sciences have elaborated the differing meanings of masculinity over time (history), across cultures (anthropology), over the course of a man's life (developmental psychology), and within any one culture among different social groups (sociology). Masculinity, in this respect, is not a constant, universal essence, but rather a dynamic fluid collection of meanings and behaviours that vary dramatically. Thus, we speak of masculinities, in recognition of the different definitions of manhood that we construct. By pluralizing the term, we acknowledge that masculinity means different things to different groups of men at different times.

Not only does a man experience his own masculinity differently over time, but the historical context in which the man is embedded cannot be ignored. In early American history, men's status used to be defined by their property ownership. By the 1930s, it was clear society deemed a man's role in life was to be a good provider to his family. The notions of work and masculinity were firmly intertwined in a cultural discourse that was affirmed by both government and business. Although the notion of the breadwinner continues today, its heyday was in the 1950s where middle-class men fulfilled this role by being "respectable" men through providing financially for their family. Alternatively, working-class masculinity displayed "rough masculinity" by engaging in drinking and rowdiness, while earning respectability by earning middle-class wages (Meyer 2001). While these dominant discourses of masculinity in the first half of the 20th century are important, it is also useful to understand that during the 1920s and 1930s, there was an undercurrent of an alternative type of man. This new man was embodied by the Peter Pan ethos and represented the seeds of a new type of masculinity, where men wanted to engage in a never-ending childhood of play, games, thrills, and personal satisfaction through the consumption of goods. This undercurrent later built the foundation for what became known in the 1950s and 1960s as the "playboy" ethic. Unlike his breadwinner countertype, this man was self-indulgent, consumption-driven, and resisted the reins of domesticity (Osgerby 2001). While the outward appearance of this "playboy" changed over time, this consumption continued through the 1980s, with the "yuppie" lifestyle, and still continues today. While past notions of masculinity dominated during certain historical eras, the most significant difference with regard to notions of masculinity at the end of the 20th century is that it was strikingly different from earlier conceptions due to its fragmented nature (Beynon 2002). In short, men's experiences of masculinity are historically placed.

Exploring Masculinity/Masculinities

Masculinity' is composed of much masculinity, for, while all men have the male body in common, there are numerous forms and expressions of gender, of 'being masculine' and 'being feminine'. Masculinity is always calculated by cultural, historical and geographical location and in our time the combined influence of feminism and the gay movement has eroded the thought of a uniform masculinity and even sexuality is no longer held to be fixed or inherent. Consequently, it is becoming ever more fashionable to use the term 'masculinities' both to reflect our new times and to divulge the cultural construction and expression of masculinity to closer and more demanding critical examination. It is hardly astonishing that when first met, the plural form surprises because it negates the accepted, commonsensical supposition that masculinity is a standardized container, fixed by biology, into which all 'normal' men are placed, something 'natural' that can even be measured in terms of psychological traits and physical attributes. However, when masculinity is connected to culture it immediately becomes apparent that in terms of enactment masculinity is a varied, mobile and fluctuating construction. Hence, masculinity can be perceived not as signifying uniformity but, on the contrary, diversity and fragmentation. If 'being male' is considered anatomical, masculinity is most certainly social, cultural and historical, "something for the girls as much as the boys and, over time, it must surely come to have no special connection to either biological sex," remarks MacInnes (MacInnes 1998: 45). Masculinity reflects social and cultural expectations of male behaviour rather than biology: In short men are not 'puppet' of their hormones. Male aggression is not conditional upon testosterone; young boys with very little testosterone can be aggressive in certain social situations and there is evidence that testosterone levels are not significantly higher in those males who are violent and abusive towards women. Furthermore, females can exhibit dominant and aggressive behaviours, and their testosterone levels are significantly lower than those of males. It is, therefore, important to distinguish between masculinity and hormone influenced behaviour. Masculinity is a set of fluid social and cultural performances and as such is not a product in the first-instance, of our hormonal state. Aggression and violence are more likely to be carried out by males, but not all males are violent and aggressive (see Hearn 1998, for discussion).

If 'maleness' is biological, then 'masculinity' is cultural. Indeed, masculinity can never float free of culture: on the contrary, it is the child of culture, shaped and expressed differently at different times in different circumstances in different places by individuals and groups (Berger et al. 1995). Men are not born with masculinity as part of their genetic make-up; rather it is something into which they are acculturated and which is composed of social codes of behaviour which they learn to reproduce in culturally appropriate ways. It is indexical of class, subculture, age and ethnicity, among other factors. Indeed, men globally have never shared the same conception of masculinity: as anthropology demonstrates, it is interpreted, enacted and experienced in culturally specific ways (Franklin 1984; Gilmore 1990; Cornwall and Lindisfarne 1994). Also, very different versions of masculinity can coexist within the same setting as has been evident even in my own occasional excursions into field settings like schools (Beynon 1985, 1989, 1993), hospitals (Beynon 1987) and prisons (Thurston and Beynon 1995; Beynon, 1996, 2001). Likewise, Cornwall and Lindisfarne (1994) reject any notion of a fixed masculine essence, pointing instead to masculinity's multiple and ambiguous meanings, meanings which alter according to context and over time. They talk of cultural borrowings and comment that 'masculinities imported from elsewhere are conflated with local ideas to produce new configurations' (Cornwall and Lindisfarne 1994: 12). But not everyone, however, is happy with the term 'masculinities'. For MacInnes (1998) its ever-widening adoption is an irrelevance which solves nothing and may even create a whole new raft of confusions. He argues that masculinity exists in the first place only as a fantasy about what men should be like, a chimerical construction to help people order and make sense of their lives. Shifting to the plural form makes absolutely no difference, therefore, since "just as there is no such thing as masculinity, neither are there any such things as masculinities" (MacInnes 1998: 40).

R.W. Connell's analysis of the practices and relations that construct the main patterns of masculinity in the current Western gender order are quite revealing. Connell goes on to describe the relation among the multiple masculinities: Hegemony, Subordination, Complicity and Marginalization. Firstly, the concept of hegemony deriving from Antonio Gramsci's analysis of class relations refers to the cultural dynamic by which a group claims and sustains a leading position in social life. At any given time, one form of masculinity rather than others is culturally exalted. Hegemonic Masculinity can be defined as the configuration of gender practice which embodies the currently accepted answer to the problem of the legitimacy of patriarchy, which guarantees the dominant position of men and the subordination of women (Connell 2005: 77). Hence, the dominant people constitute the hegemonic masculinity. Hegemonic masculinity embodies a 'currently accepted strategy'. When conditions for the defence of patriarchy change, the bases for the dominance of a particular masculinity are eroded. New groups may challenge old solutions and construct a new hegemony. The dominance of any group of men may be challenged by women. Thus, the ebb and flow of hegemony is a key element of the picture of masculinity. Secondly, as we all know, Hegemony relates to cultural dominance in the society as a whole. Within that overall framework there are specific gender relations of dominance and subordination between groups of men. Men run the risk of subordination when they do not practise gender consistent with the hegemonic system and ideology. The most important case in contemporary European/ American society is the dominance of heterosexual men and the subordination of homosexual men. This is much more than a cultural stigmatization of homosexuality or gay identity. Gay men are subordinated to straight men by an array of quite material practices. Thirdly, men who are connected with the hegemonic project but do not embody hegemonic masculinity display a relationship of complicity with the hegemonic project. Masculinities constructed in ways that realize the patriarchal dividend, without the tensions or risks of being the frontline troops of patriarchy, are complicit in this sense. Most men fall within the third category, complicit. These men accept and participate in the system of hegemonic masculinity so as to enjoy the material, physical and symbolic benefits of the subordination of women, through fantasy experience the sense of hegemony and learn to take pleasure in it, and avoid subordination marriage, fatherhood and community life often involve extensive compromises with women rather than naked domination or an uncontested display of authority. A great many men who draw the patriarchal dividend also respect their wives and mothers, are never violent towards women, do their accustomed share of the housework, bring home the family wage, and can easily convince themselves that feminists must be bra-burning extremists. Lastly, masculinities are redefined by a social dynamic in which class and gender relations are simultaneously in play. Marginalised men are those who cannot even aspire to hegemony, most often men of colour and men with disabilities. Race relations may also become an important part of the dynamic between masculinities. In a white-supremacist context, for example, black masculinities play symbolic roles for white gender construction. Marginalization therefore implies the relation between the masculinities in dominant and subordinate classes.

The social and cultural changes of the last thirty years, conventional certainties of gender have been disrupted by technological changes, economic restructuring, gay culture, the AIDS epidemic, and most importantly, by a generation of feminists, who have questioned the cultural and political supremacy of men and established that gender, like class, is a social construction. Whatever be their response to gender dislocation, men, have to confront the issue of their gender. To begin with, the apparent security of a 'normative' masculinity has been scoured as masculinity is decentred from claims to universality and rendered visible as a gender. Secondly, feminists have attacked masculinity by holding it responsible for war, sexual violence, pornography, environmental devastation and economic exploitation, the 'masculine' appears an increasingly vitiated realm. Thirdly, masculinity has become an openly contested site, revealing the differences within masculinity and the gendered nature of relations between men. The fluctuation of contemporary gender relations contains the possibilities for completely rethinking masculinity. Thus, we see that, throughout the period of contemporary gender dislocation, male culture and masculinity have been granted a central critical focus.

Femininity/Masculinity

It is increasingly recognized that feminist theories have not only constituted a most influential scholarship within academia, they have also had a profound impact on the subjectivities of countless numbers of women worldwide. This has led to immense personal and political transformations, the consequences and direction of which are still unfolding. Recognizing such, we would go so far as to suggest that feminism was the single most powerful political discourse of the twentieth century shaping up to have an even greater impact in the twenty-first. Since the challenge of feminism to the predominant patriarchal outlook on the world, modern man feels displaced, and a plaintive note has entered the discourse on gender. The problem is not only discussed on an academic level but has become part of popular culture. Role models for men have become as varied as they have been for women since the emergence of feminism. The concept of 'masculinities,' informed by recent feminist thought and the women's movement, has emerged as a means of renewing feminist discourse by encouraging a more relational approach to masculinities and femininities. This also allows for the investigation, problematization and interrogation of masculinity equally with femininity. Notwithstanding these enabling possibilities, however, "gender" is still essentially deployed in contemporary social science discourse as a synonym for women, its relational aspect obscured and the invitation to interrogate masculinities largely ignored. This is unfortunate because a textured understanding of the diversity of South Asian men's experiences, attitudes, beliefs, practices, situations, sexualities and institutions is essential to not only challenging the social dominance of men over women but for building a more humane world. The whole notion of masculinity studies may conjure up images of masculine protests to women's studies and feminism in general and, more specifically, images expressing a need on the part of some men to reassert masculine privilege in the face of women's critiques of gender relationships in society. However, masculinity studies offer a very different approach—one that does not fight with feminism but complements and extends feminism even as it challenges some feminist premises. Thus, masculinity studies are a significant outgrowth of feminist studies and an ally to its older sister in a complex and constantly shifting relationship. In her introduction to *Masculinity Studies and Feminist Theory: New Directions* (Gardiner 2002). Judith Kegan Gardiner explains what masculinity has to do with feminism and therefore also explains masculinity studies' responsibility to feminism: while the two may at first appear antagonistic, they are ultimately now dependent on one another, for better or worse. She writes: "Talk of a masculinity crisis frequently implicates feminism, and this language of crisis extends, as well, to feminist and gender theories. These arousals of anxiety depend reciprocally on each other. Feminists are anxious that after generations of struggle not enough has changed: sexism, male-dominance, and traditional masculinity still hold sway. Conversely, the media frets that American culture has changed too much, so that men's masculinity is undermined and social stability therefore imperiled" (Gardiner 2006: 6). The groundbreaking efforts of feminist scholars over the past three decades have established that development is an uneven process, not only within and between nations, but also between the sexes. Women and men are differently situated culturally and economically, with unequal access to material and cultural resources, different and unequal relationships to the provision and consumption of material goods, and different and unequal access to the political process that guides economic development. New directions in feminist studies have begun to take up this problem of rethinking masculinity. Hence, provoked by feminist studies, debates and researches on masculinity have now appeared in all the social sciences and in all the regions of the world. In the last twenty years a good deal of research has taken place on the social construction of masculinity and on men's locations and practices in gender relations.

Just as feminist theory has moved through the first, second and now third waves of critical inquiry (Farganis 1994) so has the sociology of masculinity. It is an area of sociology that has, since the mid-1950s, drawn on many theories, including structural functionalism, Marxism, psychoanalysis, critical structuralism, and, more recently, post-structuralism and theories of the post-modern. The first of these waves was concerned with the problems of male role performance and the cost to men of attempting to strictly adhere to dominant expectations of masculine ideology; what Joseph Pleck (1995) has termed "male gender role 'discrepancy'". The second wave arose in the early 1980s and sought to highlight, not so much the cost to men of patriarchy, but the centrality of male power to dominant ways of being a man. Exemplified by the work of Carrigan, Connell and Lee (1985), second-wave theorizing introduced the concept of 'hegemonic masculinity', and in so doing firmly placed masculinity as a political, multiple, contested, yet powerful concept. The third wave within the sociology of masculinity has been primarily influenced by feminist post-structuralism and theories of post-modernity (Butler 1990; Nicholson 1990). However, unlike feminist theories, which can be traced back at least to the eighteenth-century writings of Mary Wollstonecraft (Tong 1993; see also Rendall 1985), the sociology of masculinity is relatively recent, only coming into being in the latter half of the twentieth century. Since the 1950s, the USA has proved to be an especially fertile ground for research into men, with the studies undertaken by Pleck (1976), Hacker (1957), Hartley (1959), and David and Brannon (1976) being particularly influential in the early stages of the genre's development. In recognizing the importance of US scholarship in this field, it is entirely appropriate, then, that over half of the twenty-one chapters in this volume originate from North America. Profeminist men argued that men should support feminism because most are harmed by idealizing the characteristics of socially powerful men and by defining the masculine in opposition to women and subordinate men, especially homosexuals and men of colour.

Masculinity in Crisis

The issue of changing masculinities is, however, probably the key one in terms of understanding changing men and a possible crisis in masculinity. One can find numerous examples of how traditional notions of masculinity have moved out of fashion across the Western world. One can find numerous examples of how traditional notions of masculinity have moved out of fashion across the Western world. But then, masculinities have always been subject to fashion. Indeed, it can be argued that perceived notions of how males should perform their gender have never been more subject to media and popular interpretation than they are in this global, post-modern age (see Gutterman, Ch. 3). Yet, as the studies undertaken by Segal (Ch. 10), Wood and Jewkes (Ch. 7), Barrett (Ch. 4), Donald (Ch. 9), and Messner (Ch. 14) highlight, despite the evident multiplicity of masculine expression, traditional masculinities and associated values still prevail in most cultural settings. Countless numbers of men still act dominant and 'hard,' deny their emotions, resort to violence as a means of self-expression, and seek to validate their masculinity in the public world of work rather the private world of family and relationships. Moreover, such performances not only often go uncriticized, they are in fact lauded by many, both women and other men.

Traditional masculinity has begun to be regarded as 'neuro-muscular armour' that forced men to suppress tenderness, emotion and any signs of vulnerability. Writers such as Pleck and Sawyer (1974: 4) argue that men learn too well to repress joy and tenderness, so much so that "the eventual result of our not expressing emotion is not to experience it." Masculinity is presented as damaging, driving men down the destructive path of addiction to achievement, power, prestige and profit-seeking. The outcome is that many men are racked by anxiety about the level of their achievement, inept at disclosure and seemingly unable to express their feelings. Indeed, traditional masculinity is seen to be based on a very fragile foundation and what is needed is 'male liberation'. This means a renunciation of the chasing after impossible masculine goals and Pleck and Sawyer (1974) call on men to pursue instead internal satisfaction that comes from fuller emotional involvement in (their) activities and relationships. They need not depend on women for love and emotional support; rather they should use their creative energies for their own purposes and not just for others' profit. Interrogating masculinity will only make men understand who they are, how they came to be that way and what they can now do about it.

While women are breaking new ground almost everyday, we hear little about men who are breaking out of moulds. If women feel that they are forced into stereotypes, what about men? Are they not expected always to be strong, hard-working, aggressive and earn money for the family etc.? These are roles forced on men by society and any man wanting to break away from these expectations faces ostracism and is considered less than a man. As a result, many men suppress parts of their personalities, often the more creative parts, because they feel they must conform. The book, *Breaking the Moulds: Indian Men Look at Patriarchy Looking at Men*, attempts to break the "myth of masculinity as a monolithic construct and brings out the diversity, complexity, pain and richness of experiences of men who are attempting to break out of patriarchal moulds" (Ravindra R.P., Harish Sadani, Geetali V.M. and Mukund S.N. 2008). The foreword to the book is by Maithreyi Krishnaraj who says "The present book shares with us the exploration of the difficult journey of modern post-feminist, gendered man through the treacherous terrain of relationships and ideologies through the process of examining masculinity by bringing to us experiences and not just high theory.... What I liked most about the book is the hope it brings to us that there is a tremendous possibility to all of us becoming more human than just gendered beings." In the male-female equation, women are clearly the victims and the problem is clearly men. Yet more attempts have been made to change women than to change men. Empowering women, discouraging discrimination and violence against them, setting up women's organisations, legislating to protect women's rights and ensure their protection have been some of the steps taken in this direction. Hence, what is desirable is a change in the perpetrator rather than in the victim. In this context, Sadani's comments are quite revealing: "Changing the male mindset is a key aspect to women's liberation. Men also need to be 'liberated' from the shackles of patriarchy," acknowledges Harish Sadani (Interview in *Infochange News & Features*, July 2010). To do this, he founded Men Against Violence and Abuse (MAVA) in 1993, one of only a handful of organisations in India that are trying to change men's patriarchal, chauvinistic and often violent attitudes. Sadani further asserts, "Efforts to tackle gender-based violence against women in India have concentrated on empowering women to assert themselves and prevent violence. Men have been insulated from the process of transformation, says Harish Sadani of Men Against Violence and Abuse. Until men are seen as part of the solution, the status of women will not change significantly" (Interview in *Infochange News & Features*, July 2010).

The women's movement and its academic offshoot—women's studies have greatly supported the cause of women's liberation, there has been a major lacuna—men, the beneficiaries, and also in a way, the victim of patriarchy—have mostly been left out, isolated and insulated from this process of transformation. Because the women's movement had no agenda to address men as a group—to help liberate them from the shackles of patriarchal traditions and practices which impose unrealistic expectations, gender stereotypes, and unrelenting pressures upon them to perform specific roles which dehumanize them. Thus, actually, the real cause of women's marginalization is patriarchy, and not men. Men are like women, carriers (although "privileged") of patriarchy. Like women, men, too, are trapped in unenviable, dehumanizing stereotypes by patriarchy. Moreover, as experience in the past few years related to men's involvement in struggles against violence against women (VAW) shows, they can be a part of the solution too. Men can change themselves, and in the process, contribute to the change of society. Because, contrary to popular perception, masculinity is not a single, homogeneous concept. It is a social construct; and like any other social constructs, it is amenable to change. In fact, the process of social transformation cannot take place without meaningful participation of an important (and powerful) segment of society, i.e. men. While this assertion does not belittle the major role played by women in the struggle for equality, justice and liberation, it only underlines the significance of simultaneously "liberating" men from the shackles of patriarchy.

As we have already discussed that masculinity is shaped by socio-cultural forces, and we find that helping in kitchen or household work are not a man's share of work and also that the male child is conditioned not to express normal human feelings like fear, or sorrow and that is why the male mind has to banish the feelings of tenderness, rectitude, sensitivity from his mindset and create a defensive armor of audacity emanating estrangement, and loneliness. Hence, men often become violent, aggressive, and uncaring due to patriarchal modes of socialization that moulds their psyche. Images of masculinity in society are linked to being strong and violent, and to notions that men with 'power' are 'real men'. Brutality, insensitivity and ruthlessness which are associated with masculinity are, thus, creations of a warped ideal of manhood. To avoid the masculinity crisis we need to change the male mindset. It is of great importance to make the male talk and write about his own emotions and feelings, personal life, friendship, togetherness, sexual relationship, ambitions, addictions and violence if we are to striving towards men's liberation. Breaking male-stereotypes is a key factor in men's liberation.

One of the most detailed interpretations of masculinity is John MacInnes' seminal treatise, *The End of Masculinity* in which he argues that the old masculine privileges have now disappeared. He considers it to be a thoroughly good thing that has opened numerous new possibilities for men as fathers, husbands, partners, lovers, workers and so forth. Young men are no longer happy to be defined solely by their occupations, as were their fathers, certainly their grandfathers, before them. They are, instead (or so the rhetoric would have us understand), happy to swap domestic and other roles with their partners, while both heterosexual and homosexual men can now adopt an extended range of lifestyles. There is now greater tolerance of homosexuality and evidence of this comes in many forms. For example, the conservative British broadsheet *Daily Telegraph* concluded in one of its editorials that there is no reason why a gay man would not be acceptable as British prime minister. Such things mark a huge advance since until the second half of the twentieth century masculinity and femininity were commonly referred to as if they were stable, even innate, states directly linking biology and gender. Even in the recent past masculine and feminine roles were more clearly differentiated and a woman taking on a male role was viewed with the utmost suspicion, as in the figure of the resolute Bathsheba Everdene, the farm-owning heroine of Thomas Hardy's novel *Far from the Madding Crowd*. The situation has now become far less clear cut as male and female roles and values have become more similar, so much so that men and women increasingly appear to be able to choose from a shared menu of attributes (although, as previously emphasized, the more privileged of both sexes are more able to choose than the less). Indeed, when people now refer to someone as 'masculine' it is far from clear, post-Thatcher, whether they are referring to a man or to a woman. Yet a little over a generation ago it was held that men were 'naturally' more powerful, competitive, successful, vigorous and successful in sport, as well as in business, far better equipped to operate in the 'real world' outside the home than women. There still remain powerful resonances of this in the west where a tough, heroic, mythic masculinity is deeply ingrained in the national psyche, ironically at a time when its limitations have been cruelly exposed by feminists and others. While Western pop culture (whether films, records, television, videos or cyber games) continue to celebrate the 'he-man,' certainly since the 1970s there has been a strong hint of parody, even dysfunction, in the portrayal. The outcome is that many men are now upholders of a hybridized masculinity that is experienced and displayed differently at different times in different situations. Perhaps what we are currently witnessing at the start of the twenty-first century is nothing less than the emergence of a more fluid, bricolage masculinity, the result of 'channel-hopping' across versions of 'the masculine'. Narrow stereotypes, based upon biological differences, have finally been laid to rest.

Of all the current discourses surrounding transformations in gender relations that of a male crisis is particularly potent and apparent. The recent debates on masculinity converge on the question if it is really a bad time to be a man? Man's very identity, his various privileges in law, economy and politics are open to ever growing scrutiny and attack. Earlier, we had evidences of institutions where women had no entry, but now apart from the gentleman club and catholic priesthood, there is nowhere where the women's entry is banned. The earlier denominations of a virtual man comprised of qualities like heroism, independence, courage strength, nationality, will power. However, these virtues have degenerated into vices like, abuse, aggression, coldness, emotional articulacy, detachment, and isolation, an inability to communicate or to empathize. Today's man not only wears Eliot's Prufrocks' indecision but also his inability to act. What is glaring therefore is the shattering of the hegemony of the male gaze. Along with this we can also perceive the simultaneous rise of female gaze and the presence of varied representations of men, many of which subvert the older images of masculinity. Interestingly enough, nowadays we see groups of man who retaliate violently against the growing feminism in a desperate attempt to preserve their male superiority. In fact, they argue that men are actually the oppressed sex these days. The United Kingdom men movement, 1995 is one such demonstration.

Susan Faludi, one of the much noted writer on 'masculinity crisis' talks of a serious masculinity crisis in the increase of such male distress signals as anxiety, suicide, and criminality and believes that men should seek inspiration from Feminism and act as Feminism inspired women to act thirty years ago. However, men seem to blame women's advancement as a driving force behind their own distress. She agrees that masculinity is really in crisis and estimates the concept of dominant masculinity, which subordinates women and distributes power unevenly among men, as itself a cause of men's problems. The common theme within this debate is that the displays of manhood considered appropriate prior to, say, the 1950s, are socially stigmatized and debased fifty years on. Many men still yearn to perform and prove their masculinity through 'conquering the universe,' but the aggressive, dominant, emotionally repressed behaviour that such yearnings engender are increasingly seen as (self)-destructive, if not derisible. Various views are put forward as to why such a comprehensive shift in gender perspectives has come about, but most writers in this area draw on three key social markers for evidence. They assume that men are being reduced to this confused, dysfunctional and insecure state through a combination of firstly, rampant, soulless consumerism; secondly, women's (feminism's) successful assault on male bastions of privilege; and thirdly, more widespread social and cultural disapproval of traditional displays of masculinity.

Now, the question remains that how far is the issue of masculinity being in crisis true? Contrary to the clichéd statement that it is a bad time to be man, we surely can assert that it is worse time for women. Male gaze is still going strong and omnipotent. In a survey conducted in 1994 in Britain less than a fifth of mothers were working full time while the equivalent figure for fathers was more than four fifths. Almost 80% of respondents in Britain who lived as a couple said that it was usually or always the woman's job to do the laundry a mere 5% reported that it was her job to do small repairs. In Britain today, less than 3% of men report to supervisors or managers at work who are women. Otherwise too, there are umpteen suggestions of the still strong male gaze. What with the pornographic industry going stronger everyday, sexual and physical violence by men on women are becoming endemic.

Along with a crisis in masculinity, a crisis is also apparent in contemporary Feminism. Even Feminism seems to be in crisis. Despite the fact that the women's liberation movement emerges as the largest social movement in the history of United States—and probably in the world and its impact has been felt in every home, school, workplace in every form of art, entertainment and sport in all aspects of personal and public life in the United States, yet, Feminism has been described as ailing, defunct and passe today. The notion that women still have equality battles to fight at the start of the twenty-first century would strike some as quite odd. For is it not the case that women now 'have it all'? Do we not live in a 'post-feminist era'? Are not men the ones now 'in crisis'?

Ironically, despite these changing masculinities, there has been no substantive equality between men and women. Though, it cannot be denied that women have achieved greater judicial, political and economic equality than before. It cannot be denied that various material and ideological pressures seem to operate against the fabric of patriarchy. There is a gradual change in the roles of men and women with more and more women being assigned meatier roles in the social and public spheres. What is significant is that change in social relations between the sexes has been dramatic. The dynamic behind the shift is the fact that modern capitalism and liberal political philosophy devalues patriarchy and creates the conditions for feminist struggle in much the same manner as it had created the conditions for class struggle. We can conclude that masculinity may be having a crisis (Chapter 4) out there on the streets, but in academe it has never been more in demand as a means of 'unlocking' texts and settings. The sudden spate of recent publications on literary masculinities (for example, Knights 1999; Schoene-Harwood 2000) alone testifies to this.

Masculinity: Dimensions and Kinds

In any analysis of masculinity, Connell's treatise on the dimensions of masculinity is of immense significance. According to Connell, there are four dimensions that constitute this social constructionist perspective on the development of gender ideologies. First, there is a cross-cultural aspect. As the innovative work of anthropologists like Margaret Mead illustrated over half a century ago, definitions of masculinity and femininity differ from culture to culture. Some cultures, like Western culture, encourage manly stoicism and constant demonstration, while men in other cultures are even more engrossed with flashing sexual competency than American men. Still other cultures lay down a more relaxed definition of masculinity based on civic participation, emotional responsiveness, and the collective provision for the community's needs. Most simply put, masculinity means different things to different peoples. The second dimension of the social constructionist viewpoint suggests that masculinity means different things at different times. What it meant to be a man in the colonial era is quite different from what it means to be an American man today. Colonial men included devoted family men, caring, sensuous, refined, and sophisticated, or the urban shopkeeper, craftsman, or artisan who proclaimed his economic autonomy and political citizenship as a "son of liberty" during the Revolution. This contrast in models is most noteworthy when thinking of men like Thomas Jefferson or George Washington surveying their property as opposed to Thomas Paine or Paul Revere with sleeves rolled up and leather aprons over their shirts, standing at a printing press or pewter forge. Masculinity fluctuates from culture to culture and within any one culture over historical time. The third dimension of the social constructionist standpoint analyses the multiple meanings of manhood in any one society at any one particular time. Not all men are the same. Experiences depend, for example, on class, race, ethnicity, sexuality, age, even region of the country. Each of these axes changes the others. What it means to be an older, black, gay man is, one would presume, radically different from what it means to be a young, white, heterosexual farm boy. The fourth and final dimension of the social constructionist perspective includes individual development. Masculinity means different things to individual men as they age and develop. The issues grappling a man about proving himself and feeling successful, along with the social institutions in which he will endeavour to enact those experiences, all will change throughout his life. For example, men often report a "softening," the development of greater interest in care giving and nurturing when they become grandfathers than when they became fathers, often to the puzzlement and distress of their sons. In their 60s and 70s, when their children are having children, these men do not feel the same pressures to perform, to leave a mark, to prove themselves. Their battles are over, and they can relax and enjoy the fruits of their efforts. Thus, we see that the meanings of masculinity shift across cultures, through history, among men within any one culture, and over the course of a man's life. Thus, one cannot speak of masculinity as though it was a constant, singular, universal essence, but rather one must approach masculinity as an ever-hanging fluid assemblage of meanings and behaviours. In that sense, one must speak of masculinities in recognition of the different definitions of manhood constructed, articulated, and enacted in any society. By pluralizing the term, it is acknowledged that masculinity means different things to different groups of men at different times. But at the same time it cannot be forgotten that all masculinities are not created equal.

Next, we can logically move on to describe the various types of masculinities. Building on both social psychological and social structural accounts, social constructionist perspectives of various kinds highlighting complexities of men's social power have emerged. Increasingly, different masculinities are interrogated in the plural, not the singular, in discussions of hegemonic, complicit, subordinated, marginalised and resistant masculinities. The construction of masculinities has been explored in many different arenas, including: global, regional, institutional, interactional and individual men's gendered performance and identity constructions. Masculinities do not exist in socio-cultural vacuums but are constructed within specific institutional settings (Kimmel et al. 2005). They vary and change across time (history) and space (culture), within societies and through life courses and biographies. 'Masculinity' (or, masculinities') is a fictional construct. It carries no meaning outside its materialised and culturalized expression. The pluralization of masculinity highlights that there is not a single masculinity, but rather multiple masculinities, which vary within and across time, space, and cultures (Connell 1995). Further, these masculinities are arranged in a hierarchy, with the culturally dominant masculinity, or hegemonic masculinity, at the top. Connell posits four types of masculinities, more as positions in relation to one another than as personality types: hegemonic, complicit, subordinated and marginalised. The hegemonic position is the currently accepted male ideal within a particular culture at a particular time. As such, the hegemonic male is an ideal-type (Weber 1946). Connell notes that this image changes over time and place as well as being subject to contestation within a particular culture. Developed in the 1980s (Carrigan et al. 1985) to provide a relational and socially constructed conception of men and masculinities, the term 'hegemonic masculinity' describes the hierarchical interaction between multiple masculinities and explains how some men make it appear normal and necessary that they dominate most women and other men (Connell 1987). Hegemonic masculinity describes: (1) a position in the system of gender relations; (2) the system itself; and (3) the current ideology that serves to reproduce masculine domination. Connell demonstrates the essentialistic, a historical and normative liabilities in previous men's studies scholarship. In the concept of hegemonic masculinity Connell joins the constructivist view of 'doing gender' (West and Zimmerman 1987) with insights drawn from feminist scholars who described the ways in which gender relations shape social structures (Hartsock 1983). Connell seeks to explain: (1) how some men succeed in making it appear normal, natural and necessary for them to enjoy power over other men and most women; (2) why it is that so many men and women participate willingly in their own oppression; and (3) how resistance to hegemonic masculinity can promote gender justice. Most men fall within the second category, complicit. These men accept and participate in the system of hegemonic masculinity so as to (1) enjoy the material, physical and symbolic benefits of the subordination of women, (2) through fantasy experience the sense of hegemony and learn to take pleasure in it, and (3) avoid subordination. The relations among the four positions are hierarchical. A man in the subordinated position suffers that fate despite appearing to possess the physical attributes necessary to aspire to hegemony. Men run the risk of subordination when they do not practice gender consistent with the hegemonic system and ideology. Marginalised men are those who cannot even aspire to hegemony, most often men of colour and men with disabilities.

The second manner in which Connell uses 'hegemonic masculinity' is to describe the current system of gender relations: current 'configurations of practice' organise social relations and structures to the overall benefit of men in relation to women and of some men in relation to other men. Connell stresses that these configurations of practice take place across four dimensions: power, the division of labour, emotional relations and the symbolic. Connell's argument is that hegemonic masculinity as a system becomes built into social institutions so as to make it appear normal and natural for men's superordinate position to be maintained. The third usage of hegemonic masculinity, as an ideology, provides the justification through which patriarchy is legitimated and maintained. As an ideology hegemonic masculinity structures the manner in which all people experience and thereby know their world, although those experiences vary as both men and women are differentially situated by race, class and sexuality. This ideology, referred to as hegemonic complicity, can be measured across four dimensions: ideal-type masculinity, hierarchical ranking of self and others, subordination of women and the subordination of woman-like behaviour (Levy 2005). The first dimension, ideal-type masculinity, is the belief that there is a single type of masculinity that is appropriate. Different men or groups of men and women can posit a different ideal type, contesting the definition of that type, but the underlying belief in a single ideal-type typifies this dimension. Hierarchical ranking of oneself and others is perhaps the least studied component of hegemonic masculinity as an ideology. Previous scholars (Lewis 1978) spoke of competition as a restrictive component of masculinity or as a barrier to meaningful interaction. This conceptualisation fails to capture the ever present intra-psychic dimension of active hierarchic assessment. Hierarchical ranking is a process in which men compare themselves and others actively and incessantly to their general or contextual ideal type. Subordination of women and anyone or any trait perceived to be woman-like includes overt and covert sexism as well as homophobia. Although some would argue that both overt sexism and homophobia have been in decline, the lingering or residual effects, often in the form of beliefs about men, women and sexuality, are quite active. The three dimensions of hegemonic masculinity as a position, a system and an ideology can be theoretically separated while their interaction and interconnections are still recognised. Those who criticise the concept of hegemonic masculinity for confusion, reification or elitism (Demetriou 2001; Lorber 1998; Martin 1998; Whitehead 1999) need to recognise its multiple usages. R.W. Connell most succinctly defines hegemonic masculinity, "as the configuration of gender practice which embodies the currently accepted answer to the problem of the legitimacy of patriarchy which guarantees... the dominant position of men and the subordination of women" (Connell 71).

Masculinity has been conceptualized differently depending upon the approach of the researcher. Bourke (1996) outlines the five ways masculinity can be conceptualized, including biological, whereby masculinity is a product of the biological makeup of men; socialization, where masculinity is a result of the "proper" socialization of men; psychoanalytical, whereby differing masculinities are formed as a result of varying socio-historical and cultural environments; discourse, where masculinity is an outcome of discourses; and feminism, where patriarchy not only restricts men but also reinforces the oppression of women. Brannon (1976) goes on to categorize ideal masculinity into four roles: No Sissy Stuff, or the anti-feminine norm; The Big Wheel, the notion that money makes the man; The Sturdy Oak, exemplifying toughness; and Give 'Em Hell, which signifies aggression. Lindsey (1997) subsequently added a fifth role, the Macho Man, or a man who seeks sexual pursuits.

MASCULINITIES IN THE INDIAN CONTEXT

Analysing the male attitudes in the Indian context, Harish Sadani remarks, "In India, traditional efforts to tackle gender-based violence against women have concentrated on empowering women to assert themselves and prevent violence. This approach totally isolates and insulates men from the process of transformation, and keeps them embedded in the patriarchal mould. Patriarchy, apart from disadvantaging women, brings with it a set of behavioural norms and responsibilities that hinders men from expressing their fears, problems and vulnerabilities." 'Indian masculinities' are the concomitant of the varied histories of the pre-colonial, colonial and postcolonial eras, and caste and religious identities. Pre-modern (classical Hindu and medieval Muslim) masculinity in India was denoted by androgyny or femininity in masculinity, however, this value system weakened with the onset of modernism in India, brought about by colonial rule; and its accompanying ideals of binary hyper-masculinity that rendered androgyny as effeminacy, and ignored androgyny as a cultural reality and a spiritual ideal.

Effeminacy or Femininity in Masculinity had not always been given such a negative scripting in precolonial Hindu society. Along with the Brahmanical masculinity which emphasized hard asceticism, renunciation and sublimation and kshatriya masculinity which emphasized a hard aggression, pleasure and good living remained the dominant contending models of masculinity, a third model that involved androgyny particularly for men, had evolved out of Puranic traditions and had been held up as a spiritual ideal by various medieval Bhakti movements. Beginning in the 8th and 9th centuries in South India, the bhakti movements which involved an impassioned frequently eroticized intimacy with God, had, by the 13th century spread to most parts of India and remained a powerful force in 19th century. The emergence of bhakti movement also coincided with the rise of in Bengal, where they goddesses centred cults especially in Bengal, where they served as a powerful site of anticolonial resistance during the 19th century. In Bhaktihood, the devotee visualizes himself as a female and there the God is a male. It is so because the position of ideal devotee is identical to that of an ideal woman for the goal of the Bhakta [devotee] was to be possessed by the male deity.

In Hindu mythological representation, androgyny is a male phenomenon. Thus, contrary to Ashish Nandy's view, Ardhanarishwara literally, the lord (Iswara) who is half (ardha) woman (nari) is always regarded as a form of Siva, not as a form that represents an equal synthesis of Siva Parvati. In Hindu marriage, when Parvati fuses with Siva she becomes half of his body, losing half of her own substance. Similarly, the iconography of the linga (phallus) is regarded as a form of Siva alone though the linga is always surrounded by Yoni, symbolizing the goddess's sexual urge. As this ideal of Hindu Masculinity eroded under colonial assault, androgyny got rescripted as effeminacy and Hindu men felt forced to reform themselves and their religion in the image of a muscular, monotheistic, heterosexual masculine Protestantism. This shift from a positive notion about androgyny to a negative notion of effeminacy is best shown in the difference between Ramkrishna and his disciple, Vivekanand. The former saw androgyny as a special goal but the latter found the androgynous motifs of Hindu mythology as a dissolute, enervating and effeminate Vivekanand prayed, "O thou mother of the universe, vouchsafe manliness unto me- Make me a Man!"

Brought up on the archaic notions of masculinity and femininity men could not accept and assimilate the fact that all human beings have within them a blend of both. Talking about Androgyny, Dada Dharmadhikari, a man who theorized and practiced gender equality much before the emergence of feminist movement in India, remarked, "It is neither ethically desirable nor possible to determine which of the two sexes is superior. A complete individual is one who has both the excellences of man and woman. A man should have the excellences of woman in him and a woman should have the excellences of man in her. Then alone is either of them an integrated individual. As a matter of fact the two are not two separate halves but rather a harmonious whole." The Indian male today cannot comprehend the changes taking place all around him. While stereotypes of "thinking" male and "feeling" women are myths, the fact remains that a human being needs both—intellectual growth and emotional harmony. The search for intellectual growth becomes pointless without emotional harmony, as the intellect will not then have a context to exist in. By stifling his emotions, man actually held back his own growth as a human being. Today, he has reached a position, where he has no alternative but to back-track a bit and pay more attention to what he 'feels' than what he 'thinks'.

Pre-modern Masculinity in India

The male attitude to women in Indian society is depicted in the ancient religious scriptures. *Manusmriti*, an important text on Hindu law dating from 200 BC laid down laws which were instrumental in shaping the characters of the Indian male and female, but ascribed a superior role for men. In the *Manusmriti*, Manu, the lawgiver states that women are weak and fickle in nature and should not be given independence (Manu, see trans. Doniger and Smith's 1991, Chapter 9). Although she must be held in respect she should be under the control of her father first, then her husband and later her son. A good woman is one who goes about her domestic duties with devotion and bears male offspring for her husband. The importance of the male child is underlined by Manu when he states:

> The husband enters the wife, becomes an embryo, and is born here on earth. That is why the wife is called a wife, because he is born again in her. The wife brings forth a son who is just like the man she makes loves with; that is why he should guard his wife zealously, in order to keep his progeny clean. (Manu 197)

Indian masculinity can be understood thus as a construct that arose out of a deep-rooted sense of superiority in relation to women who were subjugated and oppressed. The Indian psyche is strongly influenced by the mythical characters whom they emulate at some unconscious level. The ideals that have to emulate are powerful and violent whereas women have submissive self-sacrificing characters to idealize. Founded on the powerful triumvirate Gods—Brahma, Vishnu, Mahesh, Hindu mythology presents women as consorts to the male gods. Even Durga, an exception is believed to be created out of different parts of male gods (Kinsley 97). The mythical figure of Krishna is presented as possessing eight wives and innumerable gopis. Besides, despite its matriarchal origin and the initial dominance of female deities, there appeared the Hindu practice of worshipping the phallus of Siva, Adidev which initiated the appearance of patriarchal social structures. Even the Hindu epic, *Ramayana*, presents Sita, the wife of the god Rama, following her husband into the forest where he is exiled. Kidnapped from the forest she is taken to the palace of the demon king Ravana, who is enamoured by her beauty. Rama eventually rescues Sita after killing Ravana. But Rama insists that Sita has to endure an ordeal by fire to prove her chastity. Sita comes through victorious, proving she is beyond reproach. Eventually Rama returns with Sita to Ayodhya, where he becomes king. But Sita's trauma is far from over as rumours concerning her chastity still abound. In accordance with tradition, Rama unwillingly banishes Sita from the palace. Understandably most Indian men prefer to see Sita as beautiful, dutiful and loyal.

Women would also agree, although some might argue that Sita did not take her humiliation lying down. In some versions of the *Ramayana*, she has defended herself somewhat more vigorously at her husband's unfair suspicions.

Hindu Masculinity

Hindu masculinity is always interpellated with the issue of caste, which was hierarchically conditioned. Al Beruni in his *India* describes the hierarchical assignment of duties to the four castes:

> "The Brahmana must have an ample intellect, a quiet heart, truthful speech, much patience; he must be master of his senses, a lover of justice, of evident purity, always directed upon worship, entirely bent upon religion."
>
> "The Kshatriya must fill the hearts with terror, must be brave and high-minded, must have ready speech and a liberal hand, not minding dangers, only intent upon carrying the great tasks of his calling to a happy end."
>
> "The Vaisya is to occupy himself with agriculture, with the acquisition of cattle and with trade."
>
> "The Sudra is to endeavour to render services and attention to each of the preceding classes, in order to make himself liked by them."
>
> "If each member of these castes adheres to his customs and usages, he will obtain the happiness he wishes for, supposing that he is not negligent in the worship of God, not forgetting to remember him in his most important avocations. But if anybody wants to quit the works and duties of his caste and adopt those of another caste, even if it would bring a certain honour to the latter, it is a sin, because it is a transgression of the rule." (Al Beruni 103)

In the Indian context, for instance, the hegemonic masculinity that was prominent was Brahminical masculinity. It stood far above other masculinities and exercised power. With the Brahmin occupying the top position, by the virtue of knowledge he possessed (knowledge was given prime importance and superseded strength in the Hindu canons of masculinity), hierarchies of power were well defined. If Brahmins were commonly admired and accepted for their intelligence and wisdom, Kshatriyas too were a glorified species of masculinity with their bravery, intrepidity and heroism. It was the Brahmin-Kshatriya nexus—intellect and physical power—that ruled the Hindu world for a long time. The most renowned epitome of Kshatriya masculinity was none other than King Vikramaditya of Ujjain. Intrepid and resourceful, he has occupied the Indian pantheon of heroism for a long time. Prowess in the battlefield is what marks this brand of masculinity. The might, of the Kshatriya masculinity is the might of the arm. Bravery and virility are seen as the dual characteristics of Kshatriya masculinity. Other marginalized. Masculinities such as the Sudra masculinity were built upon the discourse of duty and the work ethic. But these were subservient to the hegemonic masculinities of the medieval times—the Brahmin and the Kshatriya varieties. As we have seen, masculinity is constantly being interpellated with the issues of caste, class, race and nationality. It is also interpolated by cultural, historical and geographical locations.

Islamic Masculinity

The masculine discourse in the Islamic context is not interpellated with caste divisions. Heroic and chivalric masculinities are strongly upheld. Jihad or religious war being one of the strong motivating forces, as lslam commends and ratifies it as one of the responsibilities of a true Muslim, these two categories of masculinities are very strongly identified. Being brave and considerate and dying for one's faith is thought to be the ultimate fulfilment of life as a Muslim. Virility is considered tantamount to maleness. This forms a dominant discourse in many of the tales related in the Arabian Nights.

'Christian Manliness' and 'Indian Effeminacy' in Colonial India

However, Indian masculinity which was so firmly placed on a high pedestal during the pre-colonial era received a great setback with the arrival of the British colonial masters. A key theme during colonialism concerns the 'masculinisation' of European identity, and the 'feminisation' of its native counterpart. The supposed effeminacy of the colonised male (coupled with his barbarity) infamously forms the cornerstone of the colonialist ideology.

The British had categorized Indian men as the "effeminate other" by using a gender hierarchy rooted in a specific Anglo-Protestant interpretation of manhood—strength, rationality and individualism. They categorized the Indian Men as "martial" and "nonmartial". Thus, while some natives were feminised, others—such as Sikhs and Gurkhas—were declared to be 'martial races' (Omissi 1991). This concept was particularly deployed in the aftermath of the 1857 mutiny in light of the subsequent reorganisation of the Indian army. Concurrently, there emerged the figure of the effeminate Indian, of whom the educated Bengali (Sinha 1995) was only the best known of a number of such stereotypes. However, this does not imply that the British simply 'invented' certain types of masculine cultures and imposed them upon Indian culture. 'Martial masculinity' (O'Hanlon 1997) was also an important aspect of pre-colonial life, one which the colonisers built upon and incorporated into the discourses of colonial masculinity. As Sir George Mac Munn remarked in *The Martial Races of India* (1933).

> We do not speak of the martial races as distinct from the nonmartial, nor of Germany, nor of France. But in India we speak of the martial races as a thing apart and because the mass of people have neither martial aptitude nor physical courage. (2)
>
> I hate bookworms.... Give me a lad with pluck and spirit. What we want for India are men who can ride and shoot, who are ready at any moment to start on a hundred mile journey horseback, who will scale hill forts with a handful of men, remarked G.A. Henty.

Glorifying the Christian manliness, Smiles remarked:

> The native strength and soundness of the English race, and of manly English training and discipline, were never more powerfully exhibited, and it was there emphatically proved that Men of England are, after all, its greatest products. (Smiles 1879)

Smiles further comments:

> India has, during the last century, been a great field for the display of British energy. From Clive to Havelock and Clyde there is a long and honorable roll of distinguished names in Indian legislation and warfare—such as Wellesley, Metcalfe, Outram, Edwardes, and the Lawrences. (Smiles 231)

For the British India was full of effeminate beings:

> India has a population of 350 million...and perhaps of them, thirty-five millions whose young men are *manly* [Italics added] young men, there may be three million males between the military ages of 20 and 35! Astounding! (Munn 1933: 3)

Apart from the martial races, British were rather contemptuous of the effeminate Hindus:

> The (Hindoos) are in an awful fright and today most of the shops are shut. It is really a most despicable race, and without exaggeration...[they] have not even the pluck of a mouse.

The most potent symbol of Hindu effeminacy was the Bengali. Many critics like Mrinalini Sinha (1995) and Chowdhury (2001) have mentioned about the effeminate Bengali Babu as opposed to the hardy, masculine, imperial British ruler. Commenting on Bengalees, Macaulay remarked, "The physical organization of the Bengalee is feeble even to effeminacy.... During many ages he has been trampled upon by men of bolder and more hardy breeds" (Lord 1931: 109-10).

Macaulay's (Lord, 1931) remarks are revealing in this context:

> The race by whom this rich tract was peopled, enervated by a soft climate and accustomed to peaceful avocations, bore the same relation to other Asiatics which the Asiatics generally bear to the bold and energetic children of Europe.... Whatever the Bengalee does, he does languidly.... He shrinks from bodily exertion; ...and scarcely ever enlists as a soldier. We doubt whether there

> be a hundred genuine Bengalee in the whole army of the East India Company. (31)

Macaulay's eloquent observations about the effeminate inhabitants of Bengal were widely shared by subsequent generations of Anglo-Indians. As Mrinalini Sinha points out that the notions of effeminacy was on one hand restricted to quite specifically the Bengali "Babus" while on the other hand, it was elaborated to include the politically discontented middle class all over India. The word 'babu' underwent a change reflecting a rearticulation of colonial racial politics in changed material conditions from being used as a title of respect began to connote a social climbing, money grabbing mentality. Finally in the late 19th century, it came to signify "the grandiose pretensions and economic impotence of the potentially disloyal Anglicized or English educated Indian. Sinha quotes The Hobson Jobson, a glossary of words and phrases used by the British in India compiled in 1880's to show that in the popular imagination the word Babu had come to designate a "native clerk" who writes in English and that the word was used with a "slight savour of disparagement as characterizing a superficially cultivated but too effeminate Bengali". The stereotypical babu was thus an urban English educated alienated "intellectual".

> Nowhere in any corner of his character has the Bengali a spark of the spirit which has guided Englishman in taking and ruling India.... He is a shrewd judge of all matters regarding his own comfort.

This image of effeminate Babu signals a shift in colonial attitudes towards Western educated Indians, who are no longer seen in Macaulayan terms as mediators between the colonial administration and the rest of the Indian population, but rather as an unrepresentative and artificial minority capable of expressing nothing but the anomalies of their own situation. By the end of 19th century, effeminacy had become the most powerful signifier of India's cultural decline, and the effeminate Babu had become the quintessential embodiment of this degeneracy. Various pseudo-scientific theories came up to explain India's loss of virility. In addition to ecological factors, biological, economic, social and religious factors were frequently identified as causes of cultural decline. Bengali effeminacy was attributed to warm climate, enfeebling diet, mixed Aryan Dravidian ascent, premature maternity, Hindu caste system, insecure property relations in Hindu society and matrifocal Hinduism.

Thus, the hierarchy of martial races comprised of the effeminate Hindus and Bengalis, the manly Sikh, the devious Maratha and the loyal Gurkhas. The Britishers considered the Sikhs to be manly, active, independent and self-reliant. Ranjeet Singh for example impressed the Britishers with his military acumen. Marathas were considered to be devious due to their guerilla tactics and an unworthwhile opponent who were less masculine than the Sikhs. Gurkhas also earned praise of the British due to their military prowess but did not qualify as masculine completely. This image of effeminate India formed the basis of British confidence in their own masculinity, which in turn buttressed their belief that the martial races of India were merely exceptions to rule in a general body of effeminate Hindus. Colonial Literature of Anglo India presents examples of many native men who dress elaborately use kohl and personify cowardice. Besides, whereas an Indian male who is dominated outside home and is supposed to be rather brutal over the women at home is also seen at times to be unable to control the women of his own household and the women in purdah are firmer of character than he is and holds a greater sway over him. Kipling's shikaresque motif had greatly enhanced the idea of hyper masculinity. Manohar Malgaonkar in contrast tries to subvert the same. In *Combat of Shadows*, he shows how Englishman Henry Winton flees a rogue elephant he had been trying to slay and in the process leaves his servant to die. Afterwards, the blame of effeminacy falls on the servant while the master hides his unmanly cowardice and maintains his white man's reputation.

The colonial period also witnessed a stigmatisation of non-heterosexual masculinity. Section 377 of the Indian Penal Code, prohibiting 'unnatural sex,' was enacted in 1861 and continues to be law in contemporary India. The relative lack of censure regarding (male) homosexual relationships that characterised the pre-colonial period eventually gave way to the public and legal heteronormativity that later came to pass. Hence, groups such as Hijras became both legally and socially stigmatised. Colonialism did not, however, completely overwrite those indigenous contexts where gender identities continued to be ambiguously inflected. The example of a number of celebrated transvestite performers of the Parsi, Gujarati and Marathi theatres during the late nineteenth and early twentieth centuries is a case in point (Hansen 2004).

Nationalism and Post-independence Indian Masculinity

In the post-independence period the unfettered Indian masculinity confronted various issues like the possibility of regaining their lost confidence in themselves, Gandhi's gospel of peace and nonviolence, subjugation of low caste people and the growing assertiveness among Indian women—all contributing in the creation of crisis experienced by Indian masculinity.

Assaying Indian masculinity makes it but natural to mention the notions of masculinity upheld by the great Indian leaders during the period of British colonization of India. Ironically, perhaps the most salient context within which the colonial discourse on masculinity became codified was that of nationalism, with Mahatma Gandhi being the exception in as much as he questioned the dominant discourses on masculinity. Many among nineteenth-century Indian (Hindu) intelligentsia came to believe that in addition to colonial rule, 'emasculation' was also attributable to Muslim rule. As well, in the wake of several anti-Brahminical movements during the early twentieth century, the 'barbarity' of lower-caste masculinity became an explicitly articulated position. The Hindu-Muslim angle finds play in the contemporary politics of 'Hindutva' (or Hindu-ness), was depleted. Hindu masculinity is seen to confront an aggressive Muslim one which, in turn, must be countered. Mahatma Gandhi, as a young man, was traumatized by his own perceived weakness. He wrote, "It must at the outset be admitted that the Hindus as a rule are notoriously weak" (Quoted in Rudolph and Rudolph, 1969: 167). Mahatma Gandhi disagreed with Swami Vivekananda's masculine ideal and actively associated the feminine with peaceful and communitarian values. By celebrating the femininity of native men that Gandhi paved the way to

India's independence, thereby not simply destabilising but finally derailing the imperialist's male chauvinism.

The supposed effeminacy of the colonized male infamously forms the cornerstone of the colonialist ideology. Since the nonmasculine native male is devoid of sufficient courage, a challenging attitude or an iron zeal and is thus incapable of upholding values like achievements, competition, control, sportsmanship, efficacy and service, he is deemed incapable of controlling others. Consequently he needs to be guided by the masculine white man, who of course additionally brings civilization with him. However, in the process of consolidating the white Self against the colonised Other, the white man has to assume an almost stifling hyper masculinity. This ensures an elevated position in a world where, as Frantz Fanon asserts in *Black Skin, White Masks* (1952), he never feels himself inferior to the coloured man. His Whiteness certifies his hyper masculinity and which in turn authorizes his worldwide rule. Therefore, for the colonized Other, if being shackled in an imperialist rule confirmed his effeminacy then breaking out from it would signify their ascent to masculinity. In India's case the path to regain masculinity was paved by an unhesitant embrace and encouragement of femininity.

In contrast to the early militant phase of Indian nationalism, Gandhian Nationalism Ashis Nandy contends undermined the ethos of hyper masculinity by delinking courage and activism from aggression and violence and making them compatible with certain forms of femininity. Gandhi, in fact strategically drew upon Premodern Christianity as well as traditional Hindu images of positive androgyny and dynamic womanhood to elaborate an alternative model of masculinity, not femininity. Contrary to Nandy's view, Gandhian androgyny is neither an equal bisexual fusion of male and female nor an asexual transcendence of male and female. What Gandhi devised was a counter model of masculinity one that selectively incorporated certain Hindu conceptions of femininity for use by Indian Men in their fight against colonialism.

Gandhian ideology was an attempt to construct an oppositional model of masculinity for Indian Men rather than as an intervention into the lives of Indian Women. In this way, we can say that Gandhi's use of femininity makes strategic sense since it incorporates precisely those qualities which the imperial culture had devalued as effeminate. Gandhi used effeminacy to political advantage.

For him women were the incarnation of *ahimsa* (non-violence and love) (Rudolph and Rudolph 1969: 215). Gandhi's Muslim friend Mehtab ascribed his superior strength and athletic prowess to being a meat eater and believed that Hindus were weak because they did not eat meat. Many of the local people also believed that meat-eating made an Englishman strong and allowed him to rule India. When Gandhi later went to England to study law he continued to imitate the Englishman. But his attempts at Anglicization failed and he began to slowly return to the way of life he was accustomed to, one that was ascetic and self-denying (Rudolph and Rudolph 1969: 179). It was only a question of time before nonviolence (*ahimsa*) became the central pillar of his social and political life. Gandhi saw non-violence as representing the potency of women: "Has she not greater intuition is she not more self-sacrificing has she not greater powers of endurance, has she not greater courage?" (Quoted in Rudolph and Rudolph 1969: 192). Gandhi believed that the essence of femininity was superior to that of masculinity and masculinity was better than cowardice (Nandy 1999: 53).

Gandhi's appreciation of women is nevertheless within a patriarchal context. He wrote: It is not for women to go out and work, as men do. If we send them to the factories who will look after our domestic and social affairs? If women go out and work our social life will be ruined and moral standards will decline.... I am convinced that for men and women to go out for work together will mean the fall of both (quoted in Baldt 2000: 81). But Gandhi was also a believer in 'conscience' and the 'inner voice,' and if these made a woman flout social norms it would be acceptable. He insisted that: The wife has a perfect right to take her own course, and meekly brave the consequences when she knows herself to be in the right, and when her resistance is for a nobler cause (quoted in Baldt 2000: 81). Although Gandhi believed that the woman's place was in the home he shrewdly used them in agitations against the British to great political effect. Suresh R. Baldt argues that Gandhi realized the impact on world opinion if women peacefully demonstrated against the policies of their colonial rulers (Baldt 2000). For Gandhi the issue of women's liberation was possibly secondary to the goal of winning independence from the British. Gandhi played a significant role in the emancipation of women. His belief that women could be active in public life and still be good housewives continues to be the norm today. However, Gandhian non-violence and the glorification of the woman (however inconsistent) were slowly denuded by the rising tide of cultural nationalism towards the end of the 20th century. Vivekananda's notions of masculinity were more apt for the purpose. In promoting an aggressive nationalism some political organizations went further than Vivekananda and articulated an inimical policy towards minorities like Muslims and Christians. These organizations are unfortunately no longer marginal and are today part of the ruling political establishment. Today a coalition government led by Hindu nationalists rules the country. The seminal ideas of this nationalism largely emanated from the ideas of Vinayak Damodar Savarkar who wanted "the undying vitality of Hindu manhood" to strengthen a movement that would "make the enemies of Hindudom shudder" (Jurgensmeyer 1994: 84).

Critics on Indian Masculinity

Among the seminal treatises on Indian Masculinity, the most powerful are those of Sudhir Kakar, Ashis Nandy, Mrinalini Sinha and Rosalind O'Hanlon, to name a few. In assaying the psychological and cultural dynamics of masculinities, Sudhir Kakar probes the specificity of the normative matrices, family structures and socialization processes which shape the psyche of upper caste Hindu men. According to Kakar, the closeness of the mother-son bond is an important formative influence on the mental make-up of Indian men. A woman considers her son to be a valuable investment as the status of a married woman depends upon her ability to bear male children. In contrast to mother's excessive attention, there can be seen the negligible role of the father in looking after young children. Interestingly though, despite the intensity and ambivalence of the relationship between mother and son, Indian boys rely on their fathers to a much greater extent than their Western counterparts in the attempt to shrug off maternal dominance and acquire a masculine identity.

Ashis Nandy focuses on the complex shifts in the political culture of Indian masculinities in the colonial period due to the impact of British colonialism which propagated hyper-masculine ideals and denigrated the colonized as infantile, devious, and effeminate people. According to the British, the positive qualities of childlikeness could be found in the loyal 'martial races' of India, while childishness or feminine passive-aggression was a trait of the effete nationalists and babus drawn from the non-martial races. In reaction, Indians tried to regain self-esteem by seeking hyper-masculinity or hyper-Kshatriyahood that would make sense to their compatriots and rulers. But in an unorganized, plural society, with a tradition of only contingent legitimacy for warriorhood, such a strategy was not efficacious. This is what the advocates of armed resistance discovered to their chagrin. They had isolated themselves from the society by the time Gandhi entered Indian politics. In sum, Nandy seems to argue that pre-colonial Indian society sustained a distinctive and composite gender order which was subsequently warped through the impact of the hyper-masculinist imperial ideology introduced by the British rulers.

In a subsequent essay, O'Hanlon (1999) explores the ways in which norms of manhood informed the political and religious discourses of early seventeenth century Mughal north India, establishing significant links between kingship, statecraft and imperial service. O'Hanlon's exemplary excavation of the codes and practices shaping masculine conduct and linking it to wider configurations of power during the Mughal era needs to be extended to other ruling class cultures in the country. O'Hanlon (2007a) has also explored an earlier stage of the Mughal era by investigating the linkages between kingdom, household and the body during the reign of Akbar. Her intention is to examine the composite character of Mughal political culture from the perspectives of gender and the body.

Drawing on the innovative work of Rosselli (1980), Mrinalini Sinha has pointed out that 'British manliness' and 'Indian effeminacy' was conjointly constructed through political contestation within the imperial social formation (Sinha 1997). It is well-known that the British categorized Indian people in terms of 'martial' and 'non-martial' races. In this invidious taxonomy, the Bengali 'babus' were labelled as 'effeminate'. Consequently, they sought to recoup their masculinity. Sinha argues that an examination of the contending conceptions of masculinity, which were formed and re-formed during the colonial period, both in Britain and in India, would give us a much better understanding of the imperial social formation.

Very few social researches on masculinity have been conducted in India, so far. Recently, researches commissioned by ICRW, in India have broadened our understanding about masculinity, patriarchy and gender based violence, in Indian context. To understand the social structure and functional nature of masculinity it becomes important to explore the socio-economic bases of masculinity which is institutionalized and widely expressed as 'patriarchy'. Patriarchy is said to secure the subordination of women and the empowerment of men. Thus, women are considered to be essentially passive and emotional, suited to child-bearing and home-making. Hence, they are confined to the private or domestic sphere, resulting in their marginalisation. This marginalisation of women is manifested in domestic violence, gender based violence, sexual violence against women, poor health and lack of education in women and in various other forms, especially in India. On the other hand, men, who are thought to be naturally active and rational, are accorded a prominent role in the public or political sphere. In both the public and domestic spheres, patriarchy refers to the institutionalization of men's power over women within the economy, the polity, household and heterosexual relations. Normative stereotype of male has to play three major roles as protector, provider and procreator in both public and private sphere of their life, in patriarchal societies of Rajasthan, Punjab and Tamil Nadu (ICRW Report).

'Provider' role, in domestic sphere, is associated with men as 'breadwinner,' earning money or feeding family or providing them a social status through hard work. To sexually satisfy the wife or partner is also linked with men's provider role. The role of 'procreator' is intricately tied with masculine sexuality. As 'procreator,' capacity to father a child is seen at the centre of manhood as reflected in various studies in India including the ICRW study. 'Sexual prowess' is closely associated to procreator role. In many studies including that of ICRW and a study carried out by Engenderhealth (2006) in Delhi, Rajasthan and Karnataka, 'sexual prowess' is seen as the men's basic characteristics through which they satisfy women and also extend their control over them. Unable to fulfill the role of procreator may lead to lack of men's control over women/wife and some women may seek sexual satisfaction outside wedlock, resulting in a most important reason for violence against women (Engenderhealth 2006). Men's third normative role in patriarchal gendered society is the role of a 'protector'. In domestic sphere, the protector is seen as a fearless, courageous man who protects the honour of the household by protecting women and children of the family. Inability to do that is seen as 'unmanly' by majorities of respondents in various studies carried out in India and across the world. This protection to women and family is linked to men's control on women and family. Like a man, women should also fulfill their normative roles as assigned in a patriarchal society and that is to take care of household affaires and children and to fulfill the sexual and other needs of men. Women's deviation from their gender role may challenge the masculinity of men and may be manifested in violent behaviours and sexual violence against women, in men. The findings of INCLEN 2000 study, which states that domestic or gender based violence is a pervasive problem in India that cuts across age, education, social class and religion, can be understood in the light of above-mention phenomenon of 'failed' masculinity. These studies show how any deviation or failure to fulfill the responsibilities assigned to the normative stereotypes in these societies might be manifested in various forms of gender based violence, reinforcing Moore's writings (1995) that gender based violence is intricately linked to the real or perceived fulfillment of masculinities.

Although, there are a growing tendency among scholars and researcher to explore various dimension of masculinity, across the world, studies on 'masculinity' are scarcely done or being done in Indian context. India, as secular democratic country, although, developing towards the goals of making a free, just and equitable society, free of all the discrimination based on cast, creed and religion, as enumerated in Indian constitution, is still a country where gendered masculinities and patriarchal values stand as a main barrier in addressing the range of social and developmental issues and realigning millennium development goals. Various forms of gender based violence, marginalisation of women in mainstream development initiatives, poor health, education status and high rate of mother's mortality, along with traditional gendered discriminations necessitate an urgent attention to the issue of engendering the development process and society, through 'gender mainstreaming,' 'redistribution of reproductive roles among genders' and making 'men as partners' in the empowerment of women. Pandemics like HIV/ AIDS and growth of masculine sex ratio have, further intensified the situation, demanding immediate action with a holistic understanding of masculinities and various socio-economic and socio-political dynamics of masculinity and patriarchy.

Indian Masculinity Today

"Entangled in changes that have not been at their call or initiative, forced to make changes that go against the grain of masculine tradition, [Indian] men are increasingly caught between what they recognize as being politically correct and their own self-interest," remarked Sandhya Mulchandani.

"Masculinity is no longer what you thought it was," says psychoanalyst Sudhir Kakar. Body perfect is now the credo and vanity the overriding motive. A segment of the "new" man in today's society has been labelled as the metro sexual. In twentieth-century filmic culture, 'Indian masculinity' has been represented through the nation-building hero, the 'sensitive' creative genius and the working-class antihero who loses faith in justness of the law. With the economic liberalisation of the Indian economy, and the greater incursion of globalisation into

Indian society, consumption practices and transnational flows have emerged as major influences on masculine identity. So, for example, both the cultures of muscularity and cosmetics have, at least in urban India, found an often overlapping male audience. The conjoining of muscularity and masculinity, in particular, is something that appears to be a by-product of transnational cultural flows and the major impact of the latter appears to be in terms of body image. What is apparent today is an aggressive male machismo, inspired by the West, exercising complete sway over the cultural scenario in the last two decades. Whatever the truth, the new Shah Rukh Khan look—sends a clear signal: masculinity has turned a corner. And a new body approach is doing the rounds. In television ads, on billboards, in newspapers and magazines, everywhere, there's an Adonis—all chiselled muscle and washboard abs. Urban Indian men are not just pumping iron or downing steroids to look better. Now, surgeons say, a rising number are asserting their manliness by taking recourse to new and even controversial procedures in cosmetic surgery. The aggressive individualism promoted by the global market has also played a decisive role in legitimizing violence and a particular conception of masculinity. 'Metrosexuality' is a fluid, androgynous masculinity evident in the postmodern age. Metrosexuals came out of the closet after cultural changes in their environment and changes in views on masculinity. "Gay men provided the early prototype for metrosexuality. Decidedly single, definitely urban, dreadfully uncertain of their identity and socially emasculated, gay men pioneered the business of accessorizing—and combining—masculinity and desirability." Cultural changes, like the rise of feminism, made straight men increasingly single, uncertain and socially emasculated. The modern metrosexual—whether he accepts that particular label or not—likely enjoys premium shopping, stylish fashion and good grooming. Comfortable with himself, he's neither effeminate nor wimpy. He buys clothes almost exclusively at Mario's, where his favourite brand is Roberto Cavalli and says he "has a problem" when it comes to shopping. He once bought a $3,400 Isaia suit for its quality and cut. His cologne is Dunhill or Jean Paul Gaultier. His vodka is Ketel One.

Conservative norms, or traditional masculine norms, are, as described in Masculinity Reconstructed, "(1) avoidance of femininity; (2) restricted emotions; (3) sex disconnected from intimacy; (4) pursuit of achievement and status; (5) self-reliance; (6) strength and aggression; and (7) homophobia" (Levant 9). However, the traditional masculine norms are changing, according to a market research conducted by Euro RSCG, the fifth largest advertising agency in the world. The company conducted a survey with the question: what would men wish for if they had only one wish? What over two-thirds of the men chose was not riches or fame or glory, but love, family, and friendship. More than a third (35%) want more than anything "to grow old with a woman I love". Next was "to have happy, healthy kids" (22%), followed by "to have a circle of friends who support me unconditionally and whose company I enjoy" (10%). Only 8% dreamed of heading a Fortune 500 company, with most of those coming from the under-30 and childless cohorts (Alzheimer, par. 6). What these statistics show is that (1) pursuit of achievement and status is not as important to men as years before, as well as, to a certain degree, (2) restricted emotions and (3) sex disconnected from intimacy. The last norm change is supported by research showed that men "no longer find sexual freedom universally enthralling" (Alzheimer, par. 7). Most important shift in masculinity is that there is less avoidance of femininity (1), the "emergence of a segment of men who have embraced customs and attitudes once deemed the province of women" (Alzheimer, par. 12).

Also noticeable is the fact that the last twenty years have accelerated efforts at women's empowerment but we are also visualising the hardening of male attitudes and an increase in violence against women. Many women's movements in the country have been highlighting dowry deaths and other violence against women. A large number of non-governmental organizations are playing important roles in the empowerment of women all over the country. This has led to women being more assertive. The need of the hour today is that the empowerment of women must go along with the 'alternative' empowerment of men if it is not to lead to major conflicts in the family and outside. This new empowerment has little to do with the old brute power that men often exercised over women. This alternative empowerment must replace the old attitudes of authority and domination with equality and complementarily. This process necessitates looking into the cultural archetypes that are deeply embedded in the consciousness of both men and women. Whatever the approach, one vital thing is that a broadening, openness, is required of the psychologically defensive Indian male, simultaneously attempting to safeguard his privileges and manage with the pain that comes with creative change.

We can sum up with Michael Kimmel's remark:

> Men are changing not with the bang of transformation but also not simply with a whispered hint of a slight nudge in a new direction. New role models for men have not been replaced older ones, but have grown alongside them, creating a dynamic tension between ambitious breadwinner and compassionate father, between macho seducer and loving companion, between Rambo and Phil Donahue. (Kimmel 1987: 9)

Since there has been a "New Woman" for every new generation since the 19th century (Lee 1989), it should perhaps come as no surprise that hopeful attention would turn to "New Men". The "New Man" was said to represent a man who was more willing to share domestic and childcare responsibilities, who was more willing and able to express and share his feelings, and who was more expressive in his personal style.

In an attempt to trace the shifting coordinates of postcolonial Indian masculinities and its various forms revealed in changing gender relationships as well as the patriarchal models in society, I would deal with the relevant works of the two renowned Indian writers—Raja Rao and Anita Desai in the next two sections.

MAPPING MASCULINITIES IN THE FICTION OF RAJA RAO

One of the eminent triad and pioneers of Indian English novel, the other two being Mulkraj Anand and R.K. Narayan, Raja Rao is strikingly original. If Anand is regarded as a socialist writer, Narayan as an artistic one, Raja Rao can be seen as a philosophical-cum-metaphysical novelist. Well versed in India's past, her customs and traditions, her myths and legends and in her religious and philosophical systems, his whole approach to life and literature has been outlined against the broad perspective of the Indian philosophy and tradition. Raja Rao is more than a novelist; he is a philosopher who uses the novel as a vehicle to explore profound themes and to illuminate his vision of the "India" of the mind. Though Raja Rao is a man of great literary cultures, being equally home in the knowledge of classical Sanskrit and modern European literature, he is basically an Indian.

"Raja Rao can be read both as a writer of mantras and of manifestos.... Through seven decades of ardent practice, he has demonstrated an enduring commitment to nurturing a new sensibility in the English language," remarks Srinivasan (Hardgrave 1998: 142). British colonial discourse and the subsequent emergence of the nationalist movement in late nineteenth-century India resulted in the polarization of ideals of the body. Mahatma Gandhi inverted the dominant male nationalist discourse on the body, selectively appropriated its values, and elevated feminine bodily powers as the primary modes of resistance. Gandhian bodily practices rallied Indians to refute British charges of cowardice without having to approximate to the British ideal of martial manliness. Gandhi's vision of decolonizing the body and masculinizing the nation required infliction of suffering on the body. Gandhi demonstrated this new virtue in nationalist politics through experiments on himself: a body subject to various disciplinary practices.

Todd W. Reeser in *Masculinities in Theory* talks of "gender as a continuum, with masculinity at one end and feminity at the other and that human beings (men and women) oscillate between the two gender poles on that continuum" (Reeser 45).

Masculinity cannot be studied in isolation but only in relation to the feminine as one construct cannot exist without the other. The relationship between the two sexes has been, over the ages, one of power struggle and it is more so in modern India in which women are educated, assertive and self-reliant to some extent. Raja Rao's novels presents identities which are rooted in traditional gender definitions affirming dominant masculinities and also portray different types of male and female identity challenging the myths. Rao's male characters are mostly supporters of male hegemony—which has been defined by Connell as "the configuration of gender practice which embodies the currently accepted answer to the problem of legitimacy of patriarchy, which guarantees (or is taken to guarantee) the dominant position of men and the subordination of women" (*Kanthapura*, 77). However, Rao's portrayal of women characters presents them as taking significant strides towards emancipation. In this context the remark of Eve Kosofsky Sedgwick in *Constructing Masculinity* seems quite relevant—"Sometimes masculinity has got nothing to do with men," and similarly there are instances of masculine females, who are no less than their male counterparts in doing the 'masculine' (Sedgwick 1998: 12). Women despite being visualized as sweet, angelic, frail, gentle and domestic, emerge as crossing the gender boundaries and shattering the myths of traditional femininity. Like Gandhi believes in a celebration of femininity to gain freedom, Rao too, brings a revolution at Kanthapura spearheaded by the women characters.

Rao projects a different kind of masculinity—the masculinity of the female. A certain amount of masculine vigour emanates from his women protagonists. Reflecting manly dynamism, the constructive masculinity of these females puts to shame the inflated false pride of males. Every man has a bit of female in him and *vice versa*. In Kanthapura women perform heroic deeds like Kamala Devi Chattopadhyaya, Aruna Asaf Ali, Sarojini Naidu and Hansa Mehta. They are not only good mothers and sisters but also great freedom-fighters. Some of Rao's women characters possess certain masculine traits while other women characters are completely feminine. Those like Achakka, the narrator in Kanthapura, face critical situations and unconsciously play masculine roles and develop shades of masculine nature.

It is now commonplace to draw parallels between colonialism and the position of women in society. Bill Ashcroft, Gareth Griffiths, and Helen Tiffin claim in *The Empire Writes Back*, for instance, that women share with colonized races and peoples an intimate experience of the politics of oppression and repression, and like them they have been forced to articulate their experiences in the language of their oppressors. Rao's novel *Kanthapura* provided a liberating mantra in the formative years of Indian writing in English and establishes him as a writer of revolutionary prose. *Kanthapura* acclaimed to be one of the most popular Gandhian novels in Indian-English fiction, delineates the institutionalization of Gandhi's experiments with truth. It provides a fictional site for the testing of Gandhian political discourse on the body. The novel's representation of the *satyagrahis* endurance of verbal abuse and physical torture provides a range of contexts for framing Gandhian politics. The colonized body in Kanthapura emerges as the paradigm of suffering and as the definition of the Gandhian moral self; a site upon which sovereign violence inscribes itself but also encounters the most stubborn resistance. The novel *Kanthapura* shows how Gandhism quickly turned what was fundamentally a whole-body practice into an abstract political and moral philosophy of nonviolence.

Rao's first novel, *Kanthapura* expresses his attitude towards women. The person who tells the story is not Rao but a woman named Achakka. In the riots that culminate in the end, Achakka is seen proudly marching with the others—Brahmins and pariahs, potters and weavers, coolies and even Muslims. Though women are subject to male dominance and subjugation in the novel, it is nevertheless, the women are the one who bring about the revolution and without them it would have been impossible to challenge the colonial supremacy. Kanthapura is a brilliant example of women confronting the patriarchal convention. The dignified pedestal granted to women was only in the fictionalised world; their distressing condition became more heinous when it was circumscribed with the casteism on one side and white monolith on the other. Raja Rao endeavours such a portrayal of signifying double trauma in an Indian woman's life where her suffering on the patriarchal suppression intensifies with the subjugation on the basis of caste and race. Imagining a world of freedom and articulation, Raja Rao attempts to portray the feminine world in a very dignified pedestal beyond the parameters other traumatic world of casteism through this novel. Despite his fictional dignity, Kanthapura utters the double jeopardy that the feminine world confronts under her male counterparts.

The women in Kanthapura too, confront the colonial oppression enacted by Bade Khan the representative of the British Raj and that of the hegemonic masculinity symbolised by the male members of the family. In Kanthapura, soon after the women establish a Sevika Sangha, Najamma experiences this nightmare:

> I dreamt my husband was beating me and beating me, and I was crying and my bangles broke and I was saying, "Oh, why does he beat men [sic] with a stick and not with his hands?" and when I saw him again, it was no more my husband, it was Bade Khan. (106-07)

Bade Khan the most odious representative of the Raj in Kanthapura, merges with Najamma's husband in this dream. Clearly, the two forms of authority are not always separable—the authority of her husband and that of the colonialists—both glorifying the hegemonic masculinity.

As in any other patriarchal setup, here can be no doubt that the women follow the guidelines of their men, initially. They respect leaders, like Moorthy, and are subservient to their husbands in their own homes. Indeed, the transformations would not have taken place in Kanthapura without the inspiration of Gandhi's message and Moorthy's leadership. At crucial moments during the struggle these women look to their men for protection. After one of the first attacks on the *satyagrahis* in Kanthapura, the women rest: "And when the beds were laid and the eyelids wanted to shut, we said, 'Let them shut,' for we knew our men were not far and their eyelids did not shut" (156). As the novel progresses, the women begin to have doubts about the movement not only because of the *lathi* charges, but also because they are on the verge of being evicted from their lands. Still, they shake off their doubts, and decide to continue with the struggle, secure in the knowledge that "Men will come from the city, after all, to protect us!" (162). It's clear from these statements that women need men as their protectors, and as their spiritual and political guides because they are incapable of fending for themselves again asserting the dominance of patriarchy.

This subservience, this dependence is particularly evident in marital relationships. According to Kumari Jayawardena, Gandhi's ideal woman was the mythical Sita, the self-sacrificing, monogamous wife of the *Ramayana*, who guarded her chastity and remained loyal to Rama in spite of many provocations. Sita was "promoted" as the model for Indian women (Jayawardena 96).

Such women are not uncommon in Kanthapura. The Brahmins, for instance, talk highly of Sankar's late wife, Usha, who was "such a godlike woman. She would never utter a word loud, and never say 'nay' to anything. And when she walked the streets, they always say what a holy wife she was and beaming with her wifehood" (95-96). Significantly, these sentiments are expressed by the female narrator who implies that this "Sita model" is a goal to which all women should aspire. Such behaviour would be regarded very highly in the kind of society Usha lived in, but recent criticism claims that these ideals were propagated to ensure that women remain subservient. Maria Mies concludes: Gandhi was perhaps hardly conscious of the fact that his ideal of womanhood, which he considered to be a revival of the Hindu ideal, contained in fact many traits of the puritan-Victorian ideal of woman, as it was preached by the English bourgeoisie. When the women fail to live up to these "norms," or begin to organize their lives according to their own needs, the men use their physical strength to bring them "back into line". This phenomenon is most apparent when the women start the Sevika movement in Kanthapura once Moorthy and the others are imprisoned:

> And when our men heard of this, they said: was there nothing left for our women but to vagabond about like soldiers? And every time the milk curdled or a dhoti was

> not dry, they would say, 'And this is all because of this Sevi business,' and Radhamma's husband beat her on that day he returned from village inspection, though she was seven months pregnant. (105)

Clearly, the women in Kanthapura are exploited, and during the early part of the novel they are denied their own affairs; still, the issue is somewhat complicated because Gandhi regarded a woman's ability to endure suffering as a key to the success of his non-violent protest movement.

The significance of the relationship between men and women is neither fully explored not resolved because the men are eventually taken away by the forces of the Raj; consequently, there is very little interaction between the sexes towards the end of *Kanthapura*. The novel then focuses on the freedom struggle that in one village at least is now organized by women. The women not only use their fortitude and their ability to perform *ahimsa* to combat colonial aggression, but in the process some of their members take significant strides towards their emancipation.

In many ways, Rao's characters deconstruct the established norms of omnipotent patriarchy. Though widows in India are prohibited from participation in all forms of life and are cornered in her domesticity, Rao brings a dramatized change by making a widow, named Achakka, the narrator and portrays the narrator Achakka with this concept of evoking the confined duties thwarted upon by the patriarchal orthodoxy. Also, in contrast to the 'protector' being male according to normative masculinity, in Rao's *Kanthapura* the village protector is a goddess, Kenchamma, not a god. Her power resides in her past actions, and the origin of the village is attributed to her initial accomplishments. Kenchamma is our goddess. Great and bounteous is she. She killed a demon ages, ages ago, a demon that had come to demand our young sons as food and our young women as wives. Kenchamma came from the Heavens:

> It was the sage Tripura who had made penance to bring her down—and she waged such a battle and she fought so many a nights that the blood soaked and soaked into the earth, and that is why the Kenchamma Hill is all red....

> Thank heaven, not only did she slay the demon, but she even settled down among us, and this much I shall say, never has she failed us in our grief.

Symbolically, Kenchamma's power, incarnated in the women of Kanthapura such as Achakka (engaging in a similar battle), brings about the great social change that radicalizes the village, for Gandhi and Moorthy are only the catalysts, the inspiration for what eventually happens. They become increasingly insignificant as the narrative continues, Moorthy even disappearing from the village itself. The women are the force; they bring about the real revolution, since their husbands have had to hide in the jungles around the village. Without the force of the women, there would not, in fact, have been a revolution in Kanthapura.

Moorthy, a disciple of the Mahatma wants to spread the Mahatma Gandhi's message among the people of the village Kanthapura. In the absence of nothing else to do, the villagers start taking Moorthy seriously and give lots of support to him. Moorthy gets support from two women protagonists, Rangamma, a kind old widow, and Ratna, a passionate young widow, even the male villagers come forward with their support, like Patel Range Gowda encourages and assists Moorthy throughout the happenings of the novel. All of them together form a Congress committee in Kanthapura and, as per the Mahatma's philosophy, start mingling with the lower castes, the Pariahs. Albeit confronting scepticism from many, like the foul-mouthed Venkamma and facing opposition from Bhatta, the moneylender and all orthodox Brahmins and Swami, a local religious leader who threatens them with excommunication, the followers of Gandhian philosophy and members of the Congress committee do not retaliate from their motive of independence. Raja Rao, throughout the novel, shows the supportive villagers facing the incredulous and cynical society and confronting narrow conceptions about freedom and independence that the orthodox society imped upon them.

Among such confinement and cliché-minded society of the contemporary society, it was really arduous for women to voice their thought and opinion and moreover forming organisation was impossible. Despite all such restrictions, the women formed a Sevika Sangh to participate in the freedom struggle of the country. Historically, Gandhi actively encouraged women's involvement. In the form of philosophy of non-violence he preached, he believed women could participate in the same part as men. Moreover, because he believed women had a greater capacity for endurance and self-sacrifice and a greater ability to love, he considered they would make good *satyagrahis*. This message was what makes Moorthy bring all the women of Kanthapura together and make them aware of their empowerment and emancipation. The supportive village women gradually start attending public meetings whenever the Congress committee called for one. In her *The Second Sex*, Simone de Beauvoir analyses women can rarely form an organisation because they "lack concrete means for organising themselves into a unit". But Gandhi proved it wrong in Indian freedom struggle context for women in large number supported and participated in the freedom struggle and Raja Rao portrays what Gandhi had visualised as unity by bringing both the sexes together. Gandhi in his "Women and Social Injustice" pronounced:

> To call woman the weaker sex is a libel; it is man's injustice to woman. If by strength is meant brute strength, then indeed woman is less brute than man. If by strength is meant moral power, then woman is immeasurably man's superior. Has she not greater intuition, is she not more self-sacrificing, has she not greater powers of endurance, has she not greater courage? Without her man could not be. If non-violence is the law of our being, the future is with woman. (*Young India*, 10 April 1930)

Kanthapura reveals that the emancipation of women cannot be taken without any trouble. Definitely the orthodox and narrow-minded patriarchy objects and creates troubles and the first trouble-maker is none other than the husband. Raja Rao keeps this aspect of confinement of the masculine supremacy. So the village-women support Moorthy and his team and want to participate in their struggle but objection comes the very outset by their husbands who oppose their participation apparently because they think the women would ignore their household chores. And thus evidential truth of women emancipation reacted in staunch remarks that their conditions become horrendous in the four-walled domestic life. Despite such objections and confinement, the women break their shackles of domesticity and fight for their rights, equality and space.

Towards the end of the novel, when nothing can stop the women from marching against the soldiers sent in by the British; the change has been so complete that the women (in spite of the fact that many of them have been killed) make the voluntary choice to continue their protests. They are driven by an uncontrollable force—not Moorthy, not Gandhi—a new revolutionary consciousness.

The novel ends with Kanthapura destroyed, some of the villagers in exile in Kashipura, others imprisoned or scattered in various parts of India, and still others killed by the police. The success of the movement, as a consequence, must be measured by what the women have gained spiritually. Certainly, the narrator projects towards the end of the novel serenity and an equanimity that she had never displayed before:

> You will say we have lost this, you will say we have lost that. Kenchamma forgive us, but there is something that has entered our hearts, an abundance like the Himavathy on Gauri's night, when lights come floating down the Rampur comer, lights come floating down from Rampur and Maddur and Tippur, lights lit on the betel leaves, and with flower and kumkum and song we let them go, and they will go down the Ghats to the morning of the sea, the lights on the betel leaves, and the Mahatma will gather it all, he will gather it by the sea, and he will bless us. (180)

In Rao's *The Cow of the Barricades and Other Stories: Revaluations*, we have many specimens of hegemonic masculinity, where the fate of the women is nothing but one of passive suffering. "They all suffer and continue to exist though hardly to live." And this is regardless of their social status—Javni is a low caste woman, Akayya is a Brahmin widow, Beti in *The Little Gram Shop* is a shopkeeper's wife while Rati is the daughter of rich parents, but they all lead miserable lives. The characters contemplate suicide as a way out but their faith in God holds them back. "I wept and sobbed and often wanted to go and fall into the river. But I knew Goddess Talakamma would be angry with me, and I stopped each time I wanted to kill myself," admits Javni describing her life after the death of her husband. The unhappy Rati in *The Little Gram Shop* is kept going only by her faith in God. She is married to Chota, the son of Motilal who has risen from begging on the streets to a position where he lends out thousands of rupees but Rati lives in utter poverty: "Born of rich parents, she had hardly known what it was to do any manual work. The prettiest among her sisters, she was most loved of the family. Now her parents were dead, and her brother had never as much as written a card to her.... Of what use was all the money her husband had? What for? She had to patch her sari almost every week, and she wore silver bangles instead of the gold ones she had in childhood... ("The Cow of The Barricades" 48-49). Rati remarks, "But nothing had happened so far, nothing." The "so far shows that Rati is still hopeful that her husband might treat her humanely, but the repetition of nothing indicates that her wishes are not likely to come true. In conclusion we can say that, most of Rao's male characters portray what twenty years ago, Patricia Sexton suggested—"male norms stress values such as courage, inner direction, certain forms of aggression, autonomy, mastery, technological skill, group solidarity, adventure and considerable amounts of toughness in mind and body". In short, they present hegemonic masculinity which believes that women exist as potential sexual objects for men while men are negated as sexual objects for men. Despite the patriarchal set up, Rao's women characters are shown trying to re-examine archaic institutions that they had unquestioningly accepted for so long, and abandon many of their prejudices, and to control their destiny in a way they were not able to do before. The level of emancipation achieved, of course, is very limited; what is patent, however, is that these women who initially banded themselves together to battle the Raj succeed in initiating a movement which is imbued with its own dynamic and rationale—a movement that could be thwarted but not destroyed.

REPRESENTATIONS OF MASCULINITIES IN ANITA DESAI'S NOVELS

If the male triumvirate—Mulk Raj Anand, Raja Rao, and R.K. Narayan—can be seen as the first generation of Indian writers in English, Anita Desai, who published her first novel in 1963, might usefully be described as in the vanguard of the second-generation of Indian writers in English, and—along with Kamala Markandaya and Ruth Prawer Jhabvala—among the first generation of Indian women writing in English. The daughter of a Bengali father and a German mother, her mixed background has enabled Desai to view India from something of an outsider's perspective, to see India both as Indians and as non-Indians see it.

One of India's best known authors, Anita Desai is specially noted for her insightful depiction of the inner life of the female characters in her writings. Anita Desai's fictional oeuvre has undoubtedly carved her a distinct niche in the contemporary fictional world. What makes her remarkable is her attempt to shift the focus from socio-political realities as is evident in the novels of Kamala Markandaya, Ruth Prawer Jhabvala and Nayantara Sahgal to the exploration of the inner reality—the unexplored realm of the female pschye, the poignant evocation of human predicament and the sensitive apprehension of the existentialist vision of "anguish, abandonment and despair". In many of her works, Anita Desai has highlighted the tensions among the family members and estrangement of middle-class women. Anita Desai marked her debut as a novelist in the year 1963 with *Cry, The Peacock*. It was followed by *Voices of the City*, *Fire on the Mountain* (set in Kasuli, a hill station), *Clear Light of Day*, *Where Shall We Go This Summer?* and *The Zigzag Way*. Anita Desai's works were thrice short-listed for the prestigious Booker prize. Her novels typically gravitate around women who come of age in households heavy with patriarchal oppression, and can never blossom into their own in the arid Indian social landscape and are left gasping for air in a gender unbalanced social order.

In her attempt to explore the underlying truth, Desai probes into the human psyche and offers a psychological delineation of characters and an exploration of their sensibility. Her forte being, "the exploration of sensibility—the particular kind of modern Indian sensibility that is ill at ease," to her the "inner climate, the climate of sensibility that colours or clears or rumbles like thunder or suddenly blazes forth like lightning, is more compelling than the outer weather, the physical geography or the visible action."

In a 1983 symposium hosted by the Commonwealth Institute of London, Desai acknowledged that the sensibility of modern Indian women writers remains clearly distinguishable from that of their male counterparts. The former, Desai believes, "tend to place their emphasis differently from men" because their experiences and "values" are likely to differ. Living relatively confined lives, women writers are "more concerned with thought, emotion and sensation," whereas men are preponderantly "concerned with action, experience and achievement" ("Indian Women" 57). Like Samuel Taylor Coleridge and Virginia Woolf, however, Desai holds that "the great mind is androgynous... undivided and therefore fully, wholly creative and powerful" ("Indian Women" 58).

To her, the literary ideal is one fashioned after the Hindu mythological figure of the Ardhanarishwara—the Hermaphrodite—which depicts the union of Shiva and Shakti of male substance and female energy. But while contemporary Western literature is, in Desai's view, becoming increasingly androgynous—while such novelists as Doris Lessing, Muriel Spark, and Iris Murdoch display many of the same themes and styles as those of modern-day male writers—Indian women writers are, in Desai's words, "still exploring their feminine identity and trying to establish it as something worth possessing" ("Indian Women" 58). Although she rejects collective, militant feminism, for Desai's own "explorations" of Indian femininity and gender politics readily reveal themselves in her fiction as she attempts to make her readers "understand and feel what it is to be a woman, know how a woman thinks and feels and behaves" ("Indian Women" 58).

Desai's female characters contest the given 'otherness' to which they are subjected by the hegemonic male self. Often,

Desai's female protagonists have been cast in pejorative tropes, for example withdrawal, insufficiency, escape and removal. These images of negation, denigration and denial have contributed to a body of 'victim-criticism' on Desai's female characters. Presetting Desai's female characters as incapable of feminine assertion and identity indeed reduce them to mere silent victim in the face of an aggressive and hostile masculinity.

Indian society, which is patriarchal, thrives on the concept of females as submissive, timid and totally dependent on men. The traditional role models are placed before them—Sita who follows Rama, who becomes the embodiment of sacrifice, Savitri, whose chastity and unique love gets back her husband's life, Kunti, Gandhari, Panchali, and many others, who obey and "worship" their husbands. The values, beliefs, misconceptions about sex and gender obstruct the development of the female psyche. Women writers after Independence especially were interested in presenting the change that was slowly enveloping the Indian womanhood.

Desai's novels present a subversion of the image of woman conceived in the mould of suffering and sacrifice. Anita Desai has traced the evolution of a woman's new self in her novels. In the process, Desai offers a glimpse of the Indian male psyche deeply embedded in domination and male hegemony. Her earlier novels centre around women no doubt, but in her attempt to lay bare the inner recesses of her women characters, she also projects Indian masculinity through her male protagonists which is the cause of women's sufferings.

Her early novels including *Cry, The Peacock, Voices in the City, Where Shall We Go This Summer?* reveal her feminine concern for women's oppression, a quest for fulfilling identity, family relationships and the crumbling of traditions. Desai's fiction reveals the changing images of women in the South Asian literature. Whereas Kamala Markandaya's *Nectar in a Sieve* or Meera Mahadevan's *Shulamith* portray its positive women characters as ideal sufferers and nurturers, Desai's fiction portrays women who want their individual worth realized and break through the suffering that traditional society offers them. In her article, "A Secret Connivance," Desai describes the fate of Indian women who have had to confine themselves to the domestic scene—few women have had any experience of the world outside their homes and families. Desai's women characters may not be heroic in the traditional sense and are often swept away by historical and social forces and are unable to control them. What makes her characters heroic, however, is the fact that they show a kind of heroism of survival, of coming out through the experience of life without compromising.

Her later novels like *Fire on a Mountain*, *In Custody*, *Baumgartner's Bombay* and *Clear Light of Day*, reveal her persistent concern with the existentialist angst of a modern man trapped in the islands of loneliness. Many reviewers have praised her intellectual rigor and vivid portrayals of India, particularly her insistence on the multicultural dimension of contemporary Indian society. Postcolonial literary scholars have focused on Desai's use of Indian settings in the majority of her works, contending that colonial appropriation of Indian cultural values remains an obstacle for postcolonial writers. Others have explored the effects of English culture on the subjectivities of Desai's urban Indian middle-class characters, suggesting that the unspoken gendered and imperialist premises of colonial culture inhibit the potential growth and artistic expression of the formerly colonized. Feminist critics have assessed the psychological development of Desai's female characters in terms of the patriarchal Indian family structure while evaluating Desai's representation of the Indian feminine within the context of other Indian literature written by women. Although most of these critics have praised the complexity of the family relationships depicted in Desai's novels, several have objected to their resolutions as either too simplistic or perpetuating patriarchal values.

Most of Desai's works engage the complexities of modern Indian culture from a feminine perspective while highlighting the female Indian predicament of maintaining self-identity as an individual woman. In the female characters in Desai's fiction, we finds a reflection of the situation of women in the male dominated world wherein their growth of persons is stunted and obstructed—The wholeness which they desire to achieve, at any cost, still eludes them. *Cry, The Peacock*, Desai's first novel, chronicles the morbid dread, descent into madness, and suicide of Maya, a young Delhi housewife who is trapped in a loveless, arranged marriage to the much older Gautama, a misogynistic lawyer. The novel foreshadows several of the major recurring themes in Desai's works—the problems of independence and communication, the influence of the West, and the tensions between religious and domestic interaction. Set in the late 1950s, *Voices in the City* depicts Indian society still in transition more than a decade after India's independence from British rule. The novel is broken into four sections—the first three are named after a trio of young adult siblings from a Himalayan village who, separately and for different reasons, have moved to Calcutta. As the narrative follows each sibling individually, Desai illuminates the myriad ways that their respective social class defines their self-identities. In *Bye-Bye, Blackbird,* her first novelistic foray into a country beyond India, Desai portrays the intense xenophobia and prejudice that manifested in England during the influx of commonwealth immigration in the 1950s and 1960s. The novel opens with Dev, a young man from Calcutta, arriving in England to attend the London School of Economics. He eventually moves in with two old friends, Adit and Sarah, an Indian-English interracial couple. As Dev becomes enamoured with the English way of life, Adit becomes more and more nostalgic for his family's home in India. Like *Cry, The Peacock, Where Shall We Go This Summer?* (1975). Centres around a desperate wife looking to escape her marriage. The plot follows Sita, a housewife in her early forties, as she arrives on the rustic island of Manori after a twenty-year absence. She has brought along two of her four children, having abandoned the others with her businessman-husband in their home in Bombay. In the third trimester of yet another pregnancy and convinced that the world is hopelessly marred by cruelty and violence, Sita has returned to the island because she believes that it possesses magical powers which can safely terminate her pregnancy.

In *Fire on the Mountain,* Desai explores the effectiveness of escapism as a coping mechanism. After a lifetime of dutiful servitude to her family, elderly matriarch Nanda Kaul purchases a house in the isolated hill country of Kasauli and lives out her days in peaceful seclusion. Nanda's tranquility is disturbed, however, after her great-granddaughter Raka arrives on her doorstep, having been forced out of her home by her parents' marital problems. The novel shows the clash of generations between Raka and Nanda, the division of classes between Nanda's isolated hill community and the nearby village, and the conflict between the educational programs sponsored by the Central Government and the traditions of the local villagers. The collection *Games at Twilight* consists of eleven short stories that describe events from the everyday life of various members of the Indian middle class. Set against the historical backdrop of Delhi before the Partition of 1947, *Clear Light of Day* recounts the saga of the Das family, a Hindu clan from Old Delhi. The main characters are three of the four Das siblings: Bim, who is unmarried and teaches history at a women's college; her younger sister, Tara, who lives in America with her diplomat husband, Bakul, and their two teenage daughters; and their elder brother, Raja, who has given up his aspiration to become a poet and lives as a rich, fat businessman in Hyderabad with his Muslim-heiress wife, Benazir, and their five children. The story begins with Tara's visit to the now run-down family homestead in a suburb of Old Delhi, where Bim continues to live and to take care of their autistic younger brother, Baba. Tara has come to India to attend the wedding of Raja's eldest daughter, an event that Bim is boycotting, having long been estranged from her once beloved brother. A novella for young people, *The Village by the Sea* tells the story of a family beset by misfortune in the traditional fishing village of Thul, on the west coast of India near Bombay. With the mother ill and bedridden and the father an unemployed, abusive alcoholic, the brunt of the family responsibilities devolve upon the elder children, the adolescents Lila and Hari, both of whom have stopped attending school in order to fulfill these duties and care for their two younger siblings.

Cry, The Peacock symbolizes for Maya, the cry of a fragmented self that strives for wholeness. And the wholeness can be attained only through love that subsumes the self. Love, Maya realizes like Monisha is full of imperfections. It has the negative markings of patriarchy. Love is valorized and it is the only emotion that can give woman wholeness. Her existence can be signified only through love. This is the concept on which femininity thrives. It is not education, knowledge and awareness that can give women an identity, but love. It is the concept that divides the self of woman and causes much dilemma Maya is conscious about the negative aspect of love. Desai uses powerful images to illustrate that man's love is like a shadow, "a net" which entraps women down the ages. It assures protection but provides none.

According to Desai it is the overarching conceptualization of patriarchy that should change. It should integrate a positive attitude which will encourage women to achieve their identity. Desai implies how important the co-existence is for man and woman: closeness, the other's presence, living side by side, are presented not simply as duties, but as an aspiration characteristic of the relationship, that should join husband and wife. They may each have their roles; there is no question of their doing without each other.

It should unlock the social and familial system that keeps men and women in echo chambers. Maya longs for this coexistence, and her bitterness against the disintegration of her identity is revealed in these lines. "Don't ask me, Gautama—you can make me tell, you can talk me into anything. You can force me into anything you like if you just keep talking and questioning long enough. But don't drive me Gautama, don't drive me." The nearly volcanic heaving of Maya's consciousness is due to this ceaseless displacement of her real self within the patriarchal structure. She struggles over an explicit and habitual trick of silencing that is done by the existing system. Desai feels that "women and men function as mutual signifier and signifieds".

In *Where Shall We Go This Summer?*, Sita's escape to Manori seems to be a flight from the constraints of traditional womanhood. She becomes acutely aware of her Oedipal relations. She is convinced, more or less, that the traditional family infantilizes women and they never achieve adult ego. "She saw the island as a piece of magic, a magic mirror—it was so bright so brilliant to her eyes after the tensions and shadows of childhood.

It took her sometime to notice that this magic too, cast shadows." According to J.G. Masilamani there are two protests that she registers: "One is a protest against society and its violence...the other is her personal protest against the role her husband and children had designed for her—a breeding machine, a broody hen, an incubator" (Masilamani 28).

Sita's battles with Raman become more intense when she becomes pregnant for the fifth time. She is weary, forty years old and this pregnancy impinges on her, her limitation, powerlessness and subjectivity. Her physical condition again drags her back to the feared overwhelming femininity from which she is "in flight" to use a phrase of Karen Horney. She feels trapped. Sita becomes a victim of panic anxiety. Raman scorns Sita's escape to Manori, her eccentric behaviour and feels that she is emotional, illogical and impetuous. He feels that a woman's happiness is in the house of her husband. Self-abnegation is not looked at a sacrifice or compromise, but as a virtue. Raman is shocked when she tells him that the only happy moment in her life was when she saw a man and woman in a very intimate way, in the Hanging Gardens. He feels angry and ashamed of their relationship. He desperately tells that any woman—any woman one would think you inhuman. You have four children. You have lived comfortably, always in my house. You've not had worries. Yet your happiest memory is not of your children or your home but of strangers, seen for a moment, some lovers in a park. Not even of your own children. This outrage to a certain extent reveals the psychological abuse of a wife in the marital framework. She is always placed within the value framework. These values become integrated in systems and they endow women with an "object status"—objects endowed with a significant function and that is to become a mother, a wife and also an object of sexual gratification.

In *Fire on the Mountain,* Desai here presents the hostile environment which humiliates and batters the self of Indian women. It is the most painful ordeal for women to be tortured physically and mentally. Rape is an ultimate physical act of violence against women to control them, to dominate them. It sometimes becomes an act of vengeance. Ila Das in *Fire on the Mountain* is brutually raped by Preet Singh rapes her in order to take revenge. He tries to get his seven-year-old daughter married to a very old man for a quarter of an acre of land. Ila bravely fights against this and foils his plan. Therefore, Preet Singh retaliates in a brutal manner. Incidents of rape, abduction and battering of women are increasing in India. They are not isolated incidents. Rape is used to maintain the inequality that exists within the power structure. Women activists and organisation have raised their voice against rape and other violence against women. The battles are fought not on equal terms and unless women take radical action against this violence, this victimization will continue. The psychological trappings have become so powerful that it requires systematic counter conditioning to empower the self. All the preconceived notions about her position, her role in the family, and in society need change. The new horizons Desai visualizes are indicative of the transeffecting of Indian woman's identity. This great leap is from stagnation to dynamism.

In her novel, *In Custody*, Desai changes the focus of her primary concern from women to male figures. *In Custody,* is an ironic story about literary traditions, in which she looks closely at the lives of those who are to some extent, underprivileged. This novel attempts to look at the lives of the male characters, including Nur, an Urdu poet who is attracted by Deven, a professor of Hindi, teaching college students who are not keen on Hindi literature. Like Fernando's *Three Women*, Anita Desai's *In Custody* criticizes traditional society, but her novel focuses on a pathetic, trapped male character whose wife despises his inability to succeed financially. A terrified, insignificant person, Deven moves from mediocrity as a college lecturer to impending professional and financial ruin as he incurs increasing monetary debts, which he finally decides to endure rather than committing suicide. As the story progresses, however, Desai makes clear that just as the male characters are trapped in a world that offers no possibility for success, the female characters have even more right to feel frustrated with a sexist society that reduces them to clinging to these men who cannot provide them with what they want. *Baumgartner's Bombay* (1988), Desai's novel on a tale of German settling at Bombay unfolds the story of Hugo Baumgartner who remains a foreigner (a German) everywhere and throws light on Indo-German aspect of Anita Desai's personality.

'Hegemonic masculinity' is the normative ideal of masculinity to which men are supposed to aim. 'Hegemonic Masculinity' is not necessarily the most prevalent masculinity, but rather the most socially endorsed. Desai's male characters adhere to the codes of hegemonic masculinity and her woman characters are presented as subordinates of men be it Sita in *Where Shall We Go This Summer?*, Sarla in *In Custody*, Maya in *Cry, The Peacock*, Monisha in *Voices in the City* or Raka and Nanda Kaul in *Fire on the Mountain*. However, we cannot fail to see that there is perceptible in Desai's few novels, the trapped males, suffering as much as the women characters in the novels. We see a subversion of male attitude towards the women characters and males are shown as less diligent than their female counterparts.

A new image of woman makes prominent feministic concerns in Desai's works. Nur's wife is the representative of a feminist who explains the change that has taken place in Indian society, "Not long ago a woman who spoke about herself was considered a loose woman. To voice a pain, to divulge a secret, was considered sacrilege, a breach of family trust. Today, voices are raised without fear, and are heard outside the walls of homes that once kept women protected, also isolated. Some of the women who speak here have stepped out. Others, who have not, are beginning to be aware, eager to find expression. But let them speak for themselves." The bold letter of Nur's wife towards the end of the novel presents her as an icon of New Woman. She gains respect as a character by asserting her rights and abilities, Deven never manages such fiery rebellion. "The elegance and floridity of her Urdu entered Deven's ears like a flourish of trumpets and beat at his temples while he read. The essential, unsuspected spirit of the woman appeared to step free of its covering, all the tinsel and gauze and tawdriness, and reveal a face from which the paint and powder had been washed and which wore an expression that made Deven halt and stumble before he could read on." Deven did not have the courage to read the poetry of a woman, because she is a woman. Her bold questions point out the bias of a sexist society: "Are you not guilty of assuming that because you are a male, you have a right to brains, talent, reputation and achievement, while I, because I was born female, am condemned to find what satisfaction I can in being maligned, mocked, ignored and neglected? Is it not you who has made me play the role of the loose woman in gaudy garments by refusing to take my work seriously and giving me just that much regard that you would extend to even a failure in the arts as long as the artist was male? In this unfair world that you have created what else could I have been but what I am?"

Thus, we see that whereas her early novels concentrate on the feminine sensibility at war with the hostility of male centred universe, her later novels reveal the sensitive apprehension of existentialist against the modern man trapped in islands of loneliness, equally alienated from family and society. Desai herself speaks out in a recent interview that she has been deliberately shifting her poems from female characters to male characters. She rather feels she needs to address and voice out themes which concern males too. She says:

> Specially in my earlier work I found myself addressing the same things over and over again very much about the life of women, specially those women who are confined to home and family, also the solitude from which a person can suffer even if living within a big family or surrounded by crowds. But after several years and several books I began to feel suffocated myself by the confinement of these subjects. I felt I was limiting the territory to such an extent that it created a kind of suffocation even for me. So I deliberately opened the doors to widen the canvas and started writing more and more about male characters and their lives because I felt they had a wider experience of the world and I could address a greater variety of experiences. [Magda Costa, "Interview with Anita Desai", Lateral (March 2001)]

In her interview with Anita Desai, Corinne Demas, poses a very revealing question to Desai,

> "It occurs to me that the main two characters in your most recent novels are both men who are passive, while

the characters in your two previous novels, Bim in *Clear Light of Day* and Nanda in *Fire on the Mountain*, are women who aren't passive at all. They have control over their lives; they aren't victimized. Do you feel that men are more likely to end up helpless, or have you just been trying to overturn the stereotypes?" Desai answers that, "No, I don't think it's that. I think I'm saying that men are expected to be active, to forge a life for themselves and their families. They tend to run into trouble. There are those who can handle the situation and those who can't. And my stories are generally about those who can't, the kind that are trapped in situations over which they haven't control. I think women, perhaps mostly Indian women, have a life presented to them and they have to make the best of it. Women tend to accept the life that is given to them and to exercise whatever control they can within those parameters. Whereas a man is expected to move further beyond them—and there lies danger."

In the interview with Corinne Demas, Desai further remarks—"I don't have much patience with the theory that it's women who suffer. As far as I can see, men suffer equally."

Though Anita Desai has woven all her stories around women characters who have been victimized by a patriarchal society, she has also tried to subvert the canons of normative masculinity as we see that though Anita Desai portrays female characters who, even when they fall victim to the gendered social hierarchy, destabilize and subvert the patriarchal underpinnings of Indian society—in short, as she depicts women who "go in the opposite direction"—Desai fashions in *Voices in the City* a culturally and historically specific text that participates in creating a new feminist ideology in Indian literature written in English. As Desai reverses the Hindu idealization of women and creates subversive portraits of Indian womanhood, Desai contributes to the abrogation of orthodox male authority in both the literary and social domains.

In the interview with Corinne Demas, Anita is asked, "Two of your female characters, Tara in *Clear Light of Day* and Maya in *Cry, The Peacock*, are exceptions—they seem more like the men you write about. Desai remarks, "These two women could be said to personify the suffering of Indian women because to say that Indian society does not allow women to suffer is a travesty of truth. They suffer in many ways—emotionally, and physically. Women who triumph are exceptional—women like Bim. That there are such triumphs is another example of Indian paradox. In India you have nothing in moderation, everything in excess—and that includes paradox."

Characteristics such as aggressiveness, strength, drive, ambition, and self-reliance which are encouraged in males but discouraged in females in contemporary Western society, are evidence of the existence of hegemonic masculinity which legitimates the super ordination of men over women. The masculinity mapped by Anita Desai in her various novels is nothing other than hegemonic masculinity resting on subordination, heterosexuality and homophobia. It is used by one section of men to savor and retain their superior status and to subordinate women and other men.

The novel *In Custody* by Anita Desai is significant as Desai here explores the psyche of male protagonist outside the circumscriptions of familial ties and obligations. She makes a departure from her earlier obsessive preoccupation with the interior landscape of hypersensitive and neurotic women. The novel unfolds the story of credulous and worldly Deven Sharma, who is swayed by an idea of creating a work of his lifetime, but is unfortunately defeated by his own helplessness. A temporary lecturer in Hindi in a private college in Mirpore a suburb of Delhi, Deven is interested in Urdu literature. As the novel opens, his friend Murad, editor of the Urdu magazine *Awaz* requests Deven to interview Nur Shahjehanbadi a great Urdu poet, for a special number of his forthcoming issue. The rest of the narrative shifts between Deven's success and failure, his enthusiasm and hesitation, and the final disaster he lands into. The prime characteristics of Deven that attract our attention are his helplessness, humility, suffering and nobility. Socio-economic factors colour his personality and mould his psyche. The son of a debilitated, asthmatic school teacher, Deven belongs to a lower middle class family. As a child, he had watched closely the bitter disappointment of his mother, and the apologetic smile of his father for his failure in measuring up to her expectations. Obviously these familial and social factors generated in him a compliant and submissive tendency. Deven is one born to be bullied. He finds neither respect nor consideration from his colleagues, students nor neighbours. His wife, Sarla, is stupid, disappointed in her romantically silly notion of what marriage would bring. His idealised image of himself is that of an upright teacher in the college, a humble man in society and a victimized self at home, often turning aggressive. Deven is aware of his personal incompetence, his incapability of fulfilling his wife's dream and desires. Like his father, he feels apologetic because he cannot do better. He lives with a sense of defeat and failure. He understood because, like her, he had been defeated too; like her he was a victim. Although each understood the secret truth about the other, it did not bring about any closeness of spirit, any comradeship, because they also sensed that two victims, ought to avoid each other, not yoke together their joint disappointments. Overtly Deven's irritability and anger at his wife, appears to be the outcome of his hurt male ego. Deep down, his rage is, in a way, an externalization of his self-hate. He reproaches himself for his inadequacy to make any distinction in life "[...] all he could measure up to was this—this shabby house, its dirty corners, its wretchedness and lovelessness" (*IC* 67). What he had secretly dreamt was "the world of drama and revolving lights and feasts and furies" (*IC* 67) something like Nur's world. The impossibility of translating his dream into reality frustrated him. In society, with friends, he cannot revolt, it is basically alien to his nature. At home he imposes his superiority, turning aggressive and intimidating Sarla. Outside his home he adopts self-minimizing and protective measures. He tries to extricate sympathy from Murad by being apologetic and humble.

Deven, who has been living an ordinary mundane life, is suddenly pushed out of this ordinariness, and given the chance of a lifetime by being asked to interview Nur. The prospect opens up. Entirely new world for Deven, a world strange, unfamiliar and over-awing in which he is not quite sure how-to conduct-himself. Yet it is a world very different from the one he had expected. The world which opened in front of him, was one of 'crowded homes, of greedy poets, of the backlanes and brothel houses in Chandni Chowk. There is Nur the poet and Nur the senile, greedy, lustful man. Deven as he gets to know him is divided between the two Nurs, attracted by one and repelled by the other. In the face of all odds despite humiliation, Deven reaches the poet in all devotion. In fact, Nur the poet represents to Deven, all that he has idealized in himself. His image of Nur is hallowed by a dignity and glory which in actuality the poet lacks. "He had pictured him living either surrounded by elderly sages and dignified litterateurs or else entirely alone in divine isolation" (*IC* 51). Contrary to this he meets a senile and debilitated old man presiding over a court of louts and lechers.

Deven's difficulty arises because he lacks self-confidence, and he needs a prop to goad him and to support him. Luckily for him, help comes from Murad, Siddiqui, Nur's first wife and his students. What he does not realise is that, that each one is out to take advantage of him. Throughout the narrative Deven feels like solipsistic a trapped animal. Marriage, family and even his friendship with Nur, appears like a cage. But once when support is withdrawn, he feels betrayed. Deven realises that he has to find his own strength and not depend on others.

"Oddly enough, the certainty he could expect no more help from Murad had a calming effect upon him. Perhaps when everyone had cut him off and he was absolutely alone, he would begin to find himself and his own strength" (*IC* 189-90). Deven explores his own potentialities that he can stand by Himself. His strength lies within not without. Deven's self-discovery at the final moment of crisis is not abrupt, nor is it impossible, although it appears sudden. Deven, according to Usha Bande, suffers from what Maslow terms 'Iunah Complex' meaning a tendency to run away from one's best talent [...] or mission in life. One can get out of this situation with the help of self-awareness and self-analysis. Deven emerges out of this during his epiphanic moments. He regains his ability to take decision and shoulder his responsibility. He comprehends the secrets of trans-temporal nature of art and literature. Artistic works are not the characters of social reality, but they transcend it to project the realm of future possibility. An aesthetic experience enables a perceiver to reach beyond the condition of his existence. Art is an instrument of liberation; it cannot be expected to offer solutions to problems as science can; Deven's quest ends in value discovery. Understanding of our failure enables us to see glory in all.

Deven is torn between the conflict of dreams and duty. Murad, editor of *Awaz* is in some better position than Deven as he has not surrendered to Hindi. He wishes to crown Urdu its coveted crown. His accusation of Deven as a traitor haunts him perpetually. Whenever he enters Urdu arena, he feels like an alien. Sincerity of purpose, zest, hero-worship of Nur help Deven in no way to realize his dreams.

Deven's failure is reminiscent of Desai's tragic vision. Her novels never end in the fructified results. *In Custody* adds one more name to the series of novels which show an ultimate catastrophe waiting for her protagonists. The sordid reality of the world clashes with Deven's brittle world of dreams. The collision smashes his hopes. He is caught in the muddle of linguistic-politics. The debunking of Urdu from mainstream is equally painful to him. But his Hindu religion stands in the way to his loyalty. His meetings with Nur made him clear the essential absurdity of life and Desai's existential interpretation of human predicament. Who was Nur? A poet? An idol? A god? Or perhaps he was Deven himself wedged in the labyrinth of unexpected reversal of incidents.

Thus, we see that first of all, Deven suffers bitterly throughout *In Custody* because he has too weak a character and personality to refuse the burdens others place upon him. Second, whereas Nur's wife gains respect as a character by asserting her rights and abilities, Deven never manages such fiery rebellion. In contrast, he becomes noble at the end of the book by taking upon himself tremendous responsibilities: "He had accepted the gift of Nur's poetry and that meant he was custodian of Nur's very soul and spirit. It was a great distinction. He could not deny or abandon that under any pressure." Only as Deven decides to accept and endure whatever disasters befall him does he reach a kind of graceful inner strength: "Soon the sun would be up and blazing. The day would begin, with its calamities. They would flash out of the sky and cut him down like swords. He would run to meet them" (196).

In the same way, Desai's presentation of man-woman relationships in a patriarchal society reveals her concern and understanding of different forms of woman's experiences through an effective interplay of motive and the medium. The women in the book seem vicious, specially the enraged young wife of Deven's hero, the poet Nur. Just as the male characters are entrapped in an unsuccessful world, the female characters feel frustrated within a patriarchal society that reduces them to clinging to these men who fail to provide them what they want. Deven's wife Sarla hates him and feels disgusted at his failures. All her dreams of a luxurious life are dashed to the ground because of his meager income. But the way she registers her protest is nothing more than a symbolic dissatisfaction with her lot. It may be because of the centuries of serfdom that runs through their blood that these women fail to rebel openly.

> "Sarla never lifted her voice in his presence-countless generations of Hindu womanhood behind her stood in her way, preventing her from displaying open rebellion. Deven knew she would scream and abuse only when she was safely out of the way, preferably in the kitchen, her own domain. Her method of defense was to go into the bed room and snivel, refusing to speak at all, inciting their child to wail in sympathy." Desai is an advocate of the legitimate rights and freedom of such unfortunate women. "Anita Desai has conveyed her women characters' fundamental dependence on men through her lexicon and tropes of mastery, command and domination. Her women sometimes do attempt to assert their independence and self-sufficiency, but their quest for identity is thwarted at significant junctures...woman in Anita Desai's novel...has been fortunate enough to free herself from the shackles of femininity."

Thus, we see that Deven is heavily dependent on others, is inactive even though it may seem that he's doing a lot but any amount of action leading to no result is useless action, and has a difficult time communicating his feelings or desires to anyone. To his wife he's never been able to show any affection even when he has, he thinks showing affection will amount to losing control over her. Towards Murad, who keeps dominating him, Deven tries to undermine his authority yet is never able to speak with authority over any issue. Deven allows his life to be torn up into small, insignificant, non-functioning relationships by his incompetence toward the explicit exchanges he is invited to participate in as well as his refusal to accept the absolute meaning of what the life is trying to teach. He turns a blind eye towards his failures, even though breaking under its pressure incessantly, yet failing to accept it.

Deven's invisibility and ineffectiveness is not only restricted to his professional life, even in his house he is insignificant, if only a little less in comparison to his inconsequentiality in professional life. His wife and son are close to each other whereas Deven is distant and passive from both of them. Desai describes Deven's position in comparison to his wife and son as when sitting alone sprawled upon the broken cane chair in the veranda, he listened to Sarla moving about the house inside, and watched his son playing on the steps. It's only during angry outbursts that Deven plays any part in his household, else he is relegated to the background, both by his wife and his son. Thus, *In Custody* is not at all a novel about shifting premises, but more like a novel about the failure to shift premises. Throughout the text, Deven remains utterly unable to transform his position, location, and language into premises for hope or invention.

Thus, *In Custody* presents a male protagonist who is enmeshed in helplessness timidity and inffectuality. The women character though suffering has the spunk to react. Desai shocks us near the end of her novel when she presents Nur's young wife's point of view in a letter to Deven, in which the woman claims that Nur married her because of her "gifts and abilities," not because of sexual entrapment as had been assumed throughout the novel. She challenges him to read her enclosed Urdu poems: Let me see if you are strong enough to face them and admit to their merit. Or if they fill you with fear and insecurity because they threaten you with danger—danger that your superiority to women may become questionable. Deven's timidity prevents her defiant letter from gaining her acceptance in the world of Urdu poetry. Frightened of having to "enter that world on a mission of mercy or rescue," he tears up her poems. But her angry statements make the reader reevaluate what they previously had only seen through the eyes of a male character. By making women's frustration understandable, Desai subverts her book's primarily unsympathetic portrayals of women which turn out to have been Deven's—not the author's—perceptions.

Set primarily in post-independence Calcutta, *Voices in the City* narrates the initiation into adulthood of the three siblings, Monisha, Amia, and Nirode Ray. Behind them looms the figure of their mother, Otima and beyond the human mother lies the vengeful city-mother, Calcutta. Whereas Nirode grapples with existential questions regarding the meaninglessness of life, the nature of rebellion, and the value of suffering in the face of deadening bourgeois respectability in an ostensibly gender-neutral world, the female characters in *Voices in the City* are actively, sometimes tragically engaged in a search for self-fulfillment as women (and human beings) in an India still governed by a dominant patriarchal ideology.

Pursuing his own dreams single-mindedly and confining women to the periphery of the "masculine" world of work, Nirode reflects the arrogative dominance of Indian men in the 1950s, the chronological setting of *Voices in the City.* Conflating India's servitude under colonial rule with the Indian woman's modern-day circumscription, he stereotypes the latter as "one of those vast, soft, masses-of-rice Bengali [or, by extension, Indian] women," with "nothing in her head but a reckoning of the stores in her pantry, and nothing in her heart but a stupid sense of injury and affront," a woman who, following the country's independence, went "back to [her] old beauty sleep of neglect and delay and corruption" because of her "slave" mentality (81).

Although in his nihilism Nirode does not hold much hope for the men he knows—Sonny Ghosh, Jit Nair, and David Gunney—at least he tells their stories more fully and sympathetically than he does the women's. His accounts of the latter's lives are, by contrast, dismissive, parenthetical, or pejorative, his misogyny the result of the cultural marginalization of women as well as his own incestuous—and therefore forbidden and guilt ridden—attraction to his mother (an emotion that perhaps also paradoxically accounts for his implied homosexuality). It is, therefore, doubly ironic that, failing in his existentialist quest, Nirode finds meaning and completes his "rebellion" against the absurdity of life via Monisha's suicide. Although he claims that in the face of cowardly compromise, it is "better not to live" (18), he makes no such grand gesture of revolt himself. Rather, it is through the "excess of caring" which leads Monisha to her death that Nirode reconciles himself to others and to "the whole fantastic design of life and death" and admits the "deceit" of his earlier self-centred stance (248, 250). But even his epiphanic vision is negated at the novel's end, for, unable to shoulder the responsibility of true human "communion" and to "reverence" his mother, he sees her only as a castrating figure who has sentenced him to "death" (250, 256).

In stark contrast to Nirode's narcissistic narrative in Part I, the remaining three parts of the novel—"Monisha," "Amia," and "Mother" transcend such a rigid dichotomizing of genders to draw in the stories of both women and men. Even in her diary —a highly personal text—Monisha refers frequently to Nirode, recording her concerns about his vulnerabilities, her nursing of him after his breakdown, her finding comfort in what she perceives to be a temperamental affinity with him. Amia too seeks out her brother's counsel as she struggles to come to terms with Calcutta and adulthood. In her heartache over her relationship with the married painter, Dharma, she turns to Nirode rather than to her sister, the more conventional choice of a confidante. Despite his jibes to her about the school girlish nature of her infatuations, the philistinism of her work as a commercial artist, and her resemblance in her "feminine" possessiveness to their mother, Amia retains a familial fondness for Nirode. And in the last, climactic segment, "Mother," all the major characters come together for the first time in the novel, momentarily unified by Monisha's death as Otima reasserts her role as matriarch.

Voices in the City, in particular, can be effectively read as a political structure within a feminist context because it insistently questions and opposes the quintessential "feminine" ideal (from a masculinist perspective) rooted in Hindu mythology. Whereas Monisha and Amia dismantle the old mythologies and iconic presentations of women as subservient, self-sacrificing, chaste, and devoted to family, their mother, Otima, and beyond her the city of Calcutta, personify two of Desai's strongest statements of female resistance to the traditional structures of patriarchy. Desai nonetheless challenges the idealization of Indian women by portraying female characters who "question the myth" in various ways. Not only do Monisha and Amia in *Voices in the City* serve as counterpoints to the middle-class ideology of the Indian Hindu woman, but Otima and Calcutta as incarnations of Kali also present alternative, empowering images of Indian femininity.

The fiction of Raja Rao and Anita Desai throws new light on the growing corpus of masculinity studies in the Indian context and strongly advocates less misogynous mentality, one which would protect women's legal rights and see to their access to education and other opportunities for individual self-development.

CONCLUSION

Literature today considers "the diversity of ways in which masculinity has been constructed, enacted or even embodied" (Alderson 2006: 201). Masculinity Studies is a product of the major reconfiguration of academic disciplines where borders have been redrawn, new methodologies have emerged and many of the old disciples have been rethought and reconstituted. The common notion regarding masculinity till date was that there is one unitary and transhistorical gender state called masculinity. It is the gender representative of mankind-powerful, strong, resilient and always unfazed. As Beynon remarks "Men were expected to be strong, authoritative, decisive, disciplined and resourceful" (Beynon 30).

However, with the issue of masculinity being foregrounded in various fields of academic study, the scenario has changed.

Masculinity is no longer considered a homogeneous entity, but one that is heterogeneously composed. As Jeffrey Jerome Cohen says: "Gender theorists have argued that the identity we unreflectively assume to be our own does not arise from some central, determinate self, but is rather a collection of behaviours, expressions, and material signifiers in which we are dressed by the cultural moment that enabled our coming into being" (Cohen 2). Further Connell succinctly conveys this idea: "Masculinity is not a static phenomenon based on the universally common structure of patriarchy; instead it is dynamic phenomenon which takes different shapes and forms, which vary within and across time, space and cultures" (Connell 1995).

When we think of power we think of men and we tend to ignore what Guru Nanak, the first Sikh Guru remarked—"From Woman, man is born; within woman, man is conceived; to woman he is engaged and married. Woman becomes his friend; through woman the future generations come. When his woman dies, he seeks another woman; to woman he is bound. So why call her bad? From her, kings are born. From woman, woman is born; without woman, there would be no one at all."

Women must realize that they too possess man's heroic qualities, and must learn to balance them with characteristics such as compassion, softness, and nurturing attitude. Women must see themselves as strong and fearless in order to overcome injustices towards their gender. Men need to shed off the traditional characteristics of masculinity and look forward to the New Man who takes care of family and society along with the fair sex. A real man should be daring, courageous, confident and command respect, should be responsible towards his family and should be able to prove his manliness or masculinity in times of crisis.

Masculinity has been constructed over the last century almost entirely around the idea of men as providers and protectors, and frankly, women don't need that any more. Already in at least a dozen major metropolitan areas, women earn on average more than men. Women are waiting longer to get married, and are more often the initiators of divorce—with their own incomes, they can afford to be pickier about their spouses, both going into marriage and when deciding whether to continue their relationships. Constructs of Masculinity are changing with the changing times. The Canadian novelist Margaret Laurence, best projects the crisis in Masculinity: "I don't think enough attention has been paid to the problems men have and/or going to have increasingly because of the changes taking place in women. Men have to be reeducated with the minimum of damage to them. These are our husbands, our sons; our lovers.... We can't go to war against them. The change must liberate them as well."

One of the most striking ways in which the valorisation of masculinity is expressed in the contemporary period is through the persistence of preferences for male children, as manifested in the worsening male-female ratios across a number of states in India. The social privileging of masculinity also finds play in the pervasiveness of the linkage between men's 'honour' and women's propriety. This expresses the idea that the integrity of masculine identity is dependent not merely on male behaviour but also on that of women. Hence, in India a great deal of violence towards women occurs in those contexts where women are seen to have violated the norms of female behaviour, which in turn has consequences for male honour. In many instances, the control of female sexuality is explicitly at issue. In the present scenario, the remarks of Mangesh Kulkarni, a brilliant scholar of masculinities is quite illuminating, "The traditional dominant forms of masculinity which valorize self-centred, unemotional, competitive, aggressive and sexually promiscuous behaviour require serious re-evaluation for enhancing the well-being of both men and women. The reconstruction of masculinity along emancipatory lines must therefore proceed in tandem with feminism. The agenda set up by men would include the salvaging and strengthening the fatherhood, encouragement of healthy male-bonding and mentoring to generate new forms of solidarity, defeating the 'machine man' archetype so as to achieve true physical, psychological and spiritual well-being and establishing a nurturing and creative relationship with nature. The promotion of an appropriate set of male values awaits the emergence of a "critical mass" of men who will wake up to the need for men to draw strength from each other, to exchange passivity for

activity, and who will generate a new and credible set of roles for themselves that will complement rather than antagonize the new confidence of women.

What is appreciable however, are the attitudinal changes that are beginning to happen among educated urban men who have learnt to treat women with as individuals with their own minds and respect them. It is certainly a positive trend that promises to spread widely. A society must work towards a balanced gender equation in which both men and women are able to find their own rightful place.

Works Cited

Alderson, David. "Masculinity and Cultural Studies," *Modern North American Criticism and Theory*. Ed. Julian Wolfreys. Edinburgh: Edinburgh University Press, 2006.

Alzheimer, Lillian. "Metrosexuals: The Future of Men?" Euro RSCG. 22 June 2003. 15 Dec. 2003. [http://www.eurorscg.com]

Atwood, Margaret. "Face to Face," *A Place to Stand On: Essays by and about Margaret Laurence*, Ed. George Woodcock (1974, Edmonton: NeWest Press, 1983), 23.

Baldt, S. "The Politics of Gandhi's Feminism," in S. Ranchod-Nilsson and M. Tetreault Ed. *Women, States and Nationalism*. London: Routledge, 2000.

Beasley, C. *Gender and Sexuality: Critical Theories, Critical Thinkers*. London: Sage Publications, 2005.

Berger, Maurice; Brian Wallis; Simon Watson; Carrie Mae Weems. *Constructing Masculinity*. New York: Routledge, 1995.

Beynon, John. *Masculinities and Culture*. Philadelphia, PA: Open University Press, 2002.

Boehmer, Elleke. *Colonial & Postcolonial Literature*. Oxford: Oxford University Press, 2005: 71.

Brannon, Robert. "The Male Sex Role: Our Culture's Blueprint of Manhood and What it's Done for us Lately," in *The 49% Majority: The Male Sex Role,* Ed. D. David and R. Brannon. Reading, MA: Addison-Wesley, 1976.

Burke, Peter, J. Jan. E. Stets and Maureen A. Pirog-Good. "Gender Identity, Self-Esteem, and Physical and Sexual Abuse in Dating Relationships." *Social Psychology Quarterly,* 51: 272-85, 1988.

Butler, J. *Gender Trouble: Feminism and the Subversion of Identity*. New York: Routledge, 1990.

Carrigan, T. Bob Connell and J. Lee. *Toward a New Sociology of Masculinity. Theory and Society*, 14: 551-604. 1985.

Chowdhury, I. *The Frail Hero and Virile History: Gender and Politics of Culture in Colonial Bengal.* New Delhi: Oxford University Press, 2001.

Connell, R.W. *Masculinities*. Cambridge: Polity Press, 1995.

——. *Masculinities*, 2nd Edition. University of California Press, 2005.

——. *Gender and Power*. Stanford, C.A.: Stanford University Press, 1987.

——. "Psychoanalysis on Masculinity." In H. Brod and M. Kaufman, Eds., *Theorizing Masculinities*. Thousand Oaks, CA: Sage, 1994.

Cornwall, Andrea and Nancy Lindisfarne. *Dislocating Masculinity: Comparative Ethnographies* (Male Orders). New York: Routledge, 1994.

Danto, Arthur C. "The Shape of Artistic Pasts, East and West" in Eliot Deutsch (Ed.), *Culture and Modernity: East-West Philosophic Perspectives*, Delhi: Motilal Banarasidass, p. 338.

David, D. and Brannon, R. (Eds). *The Forty-Nine Percent Majority: The Male Sex Role*. Reading, MA: Addison-Wesley, 1976.

Demetriou, D.Z. "Connell's Concept of Hegemonic Masculinity: A Critique." *Theory and Society*, 30: 337-61, 2001.

Desai, Anita. *In Custody*. London: Heinemann, 1984.

——. *Voices in the City*, 1965. New Delhi: Orient, 1988.

——. "Against the Current: A Conversation with Anita Desai." Interview with Corinne Demás Bliss. *The Massachusetts Review* 29.3, 521-37, 1988.

——. *Where Shall We Go This Summer*? New Delhi: Orient Paperbacks, 1982.

——. *Cry, The Peacock*, New Delhi: Orient Paperbacks, 1965.

Faludi, S. *Stiffed: The Betrayal of the Modern Man*. London: Chatto & Windus, 1999.

Farganis, S. *Situating Feminism: From Thought to Action*. Thousand Oaks: Sage, 1994.

Franklin, Clyde W. *The Changing Definition of Masculinity*. New York: Plenum Books, 1984.

Gardiner, Judith Kegan (Ed.). *Masculinity Studies and Feminist Theory: New Directions*. Columbia University Press, 2002.

George, Sir MacMunn. *The Martial Races of India*. Delhi: Mittal Publications, 1979.

Gilmore, David D. *Manhood in the Making: Cultural Concepts of Masculinity*. New Haven, CT: Yale UP, 1991.

Gittings, C.E. (Ed.). *Imperialism and Gender: Constructions of Masculinity*. West Yorkshire: Dangaroo Press, 1996.

Glover, David and Cora Kaplan. *Genders*. New York: Routledge, 2000.

Hacker, H.M. *The New Burdens of Masculinity, Marriage and Family Living*. 1957 (3): 227-33.

Hansen, K. "Theatrical Transvestism in the Parsi, Gujarati and Marathi Theatres" (1850–1940), S. Srivastava (Ed.). *Sexual Sites, Seminal Attitudes, Sexualities, Masculinities and Culture in South Asia*. New Delhi: Sage, 2005, 99-122.

Hartley, R.E. *Sex-Role Pressures and the Socialization of the Male Child*. Psychological Reports, 1959 (5): 457-68.

Hartsock, Nancy, C.M. Money. *Sex and Power: Toward a Feminist Historical Materialism*. New York: Longman, 1983.

Hearn, J. *The Violences of Men*. London: Sage, 1998.

Henty, G.A. *Through the Sikh War: A Tale of the Conquest of the Punjab*. Robinson Books, 2002.

Homi, Bhabha. "Of Mimicry and Man: The Ambivalence of Colonial Discourse" in Philip Rice and Patricia Waugh (Eds.), *Modern Literary Theory*. New York: Arnold, 384.

Jayawardena, Kumari. *Feminism and Nationalism in the Third World*. London: Zed, 1986.

Juergensmeyer, Mark. *The New Cold War: Religious Nationalism Confronts the Secular State*. Oxford: Oxford University Press, 1994.

Jung, C.G. *Aspects of Feminine*. Princeton, NJ: Princeton University Press, 1983.

Kimmel, Michael. *Changing Men: New Directions in Research on Men and Masculinity*. London: Sage Publications, 1987.

——. *The Gendered Society*. USA: OUP, 2000.

Kinsley, David. *Hindu Goddess: Vision of the Divine Feminine in the Hindu Religious Tradition*, 1986. Berkeley, LA: University of California Press, 1988.

Knights, Ben. *Writing Masculinities: Male Narratives in Twentieth-Century Fiction*. Palgrave, 1999.

Krishnaswamy, Revathy. "The Economy of Colonial Desire," *The Masculinity Studies Reader*. Rachel Adams and David Savran (Eds.), USA: Blackwell, 2002.

Kulkarni, Mangesh. "Reconstructing Indian Masculinities," *Gentleman* (May 2001).

Kumar, Avanish. "Constructs of Masculinities," 23 March 2008. <www.insightresearchnetwork.org>

Levant, Ronald F. and Gini Kopecky. *Masculinity Reconstructed: Changing the Rules of Manhood: At Work, in Relationships and in Family Life*. New York: Dutton, 1995.

Levy, D.P. "Hegemonic Masculinity, Friendship and Comradeship," *Journal of Men's Studies*, 13(2): 199-225, 2005.

Lewis, R.A. "Emotional Intimacy among Men," *Journal of Social Issues*, 34: 108-21, 1978.

Lorber, J. Symposium on R. Connell's *Masculinities*, *Gender and Society*, 12: 469-72 (1998).

MacInnes, John. *The End of Masculinity*. Open University Press, Buckingham, 1998.

Magda, Costa. "Interview with Anita Desai," *Lateral* (March 2001).

Manu. *The Laws of Manu*, Trans. W. Doniger and B. Smith. London: Penguin, 1991.

Marik, S. "He for God only, she for God in him," *The Telegraph* (Calcutta) November 29th, 1999.

Martin, P.Y. Symposium on R. Connell's *Masculinities*, *Gender and Society*, 12: 472-74 (1998).

Masilamani, J.G. "Feminism in Anita Desai," *Kakatiya Journal of English Studies*, 3, No. 1, 1978.

Meyer, Stephen. "Work, Play, Power: Masculine Culture on the Automotive Shop Floor, 1930-1960," *Boys and Their Toys*, ed. R. Horowitz. New York: Routledge, 2001: 13-32.

Mulchandani, Sandhya. *The Indian Man: His True Colours* (New Delhi: Picus, 1999), 177.

Nandy, A. *Exiled at Home*. Oxford: Oxford University Press, 1999.

Nicholson, L.J. (Ed.). *Feminism/Postmodernism*. New York: Routledge, 1990.

O'Hanlon, R. "Issues of Masculinity in North Indian History: The Bangash Nawabs of Farrukhabad," *Indian Journal of Gender Studies*, 4(1): 1-19 (1997).

Omissi, D. "Martial Races: Ethnicity and Security in Colonial India 1858–1939," *War and Society*, 9(1): 1-27 (1991).

Osgerby, Bill. *Playboys in Paradise*. New York: Oxford International Publishers, 2001.

Pleck, J.H. "The Gender Role Strain Paradigm: An Update," R.F. Levant and W.S. Pollack (Eds), *A New Psychology of Men*. New York: Basic Books, 1995.

Rao, Raja. *The Cow of the Barricades and Other Stories: Revaluations*. Bombay: Oxford University Press, Champak Library, 1947: 19.

——. *Kanthapura*. New York: James Laughlin, 1963.

Ravindra, R.P., Harish Sadani, Geetali V.M. and Mukund S.N. *Breaking the Moulds: Indian Men Look at Patriarchy Looking at Men*. Books for Change, 2008.

Reeser, Todd W. *Masculinities in Theory: An Introduction*. UK: Wiley-Blackwell, 2010: 45.

Rendall, J. *The Origins of Modern Feminism: Women in Britain, France and the United States*, 1780-1860. London: Macmillan, 1985.

Roy, P. *Indian Traffic*. New Delhi: Vistaar Publications, 1999.

Rudolph, L.I. and Rudolph, S. *The Modernity of Tradition*. New Delhi: Orient Longman, 1969.

Sedgwick, Eve Kosofsky. *Constructing Masculinity.* Ed. Maurice Berger, Brian Wallis and Simon Watson. New York: Routledge. 1998: 12.

Schoene Berthold-Harwood. *Writing Men: Literary Masculinities from Frankenstein to the New Man*. Edinburgh University Press, 2000.

Sinha, Mrinalini. *Colonial Masculinity: The 'Manly Englishman' and the 'Effeminate Bengali' in the Late Nineteenth Century*. London: Manchester University Press, 1995.

Smiles, Samuel. *Self Help*. London: John Murray, 1879.

Spence, Janet T. "Gender Identity and Implications for Concepts of Masculinity and Femininity." 59-96 in T.B. Sonderegger (Ed.), *Nebraska Symposium on Motivation: Psychology and Gender*. Lincoln: University of Nebraska Press, 1985.

Srinivasan, R.E. "Blinding I: Toward a Poetics of Post Traditional Technology," in Hardgrave, Robert L. (Ed.), *Word as Mantra: The Art of Raja Rao*, New Delhi: Katha, 1998, 142.

Tong, R. *Feminist Thought: A Comprehensive Introduction*. London: Routledge, 1993.

Weber, Max. *Essays in Sociology*, Ed. by H.H. Gareth, Oxford: Oxford University Press, 1946.

West, Candace and Don H. Zimmerman. "Doing Gender." *Gender and Society,* 1: 125-51 (1987).

Whitehead, S. "Hegemonic Masculinity Revisited," *Gender, Work and Organization*, 6: 58-62 (1999).

Chapter 2

Framing the Feminine

Defining Feminism

"Throughout history people have knocked their heads against the riddle of nature of Femininity" remarked Sigmund Freud, "... Nor will you have escaped worrying over this problem—those of you who are men; to those of you who are women this will not apply—you are yourselves the person" (Freud 1965: 112). In light of Freud's statement, David Glover and Kaplan remarked succinctly, "For although femininity may be defined as a set of attributes ascribed to biologically sexed females, what exactly those attributes are, and the extent to which any given version of femininity is natural or cultural, have been debated long and hard by women themselves" (Glover 2009: 26).

Alice Jardine's remark, "We would[n't] want to end up by demanding a definition of what feminism is and, therefore, of what one must do, say, and be, if one is to acquire that epithet; dictionary meanings are suffocating, to say the least" (Jardine 1985: 20) reflects the usual mystifying unwillingness among feminists to define what feminism is. As Rosalind Delmar, in her paper, "What is Feminism?" talks of "the impossibility of constructing modern feminism as a simple unity in the present or of arriving at a shared feminist definition of feminism", because of the fragmentation of contemporary feminism (Delmar 1986: 9). Rosemarie Tong too, in her book, *Feminist Thought* remarks, "even if this is not the time to decide, once and for all, what feminism is, it is probably the time to consider the possibility that its meanings are ever changing" (Tong 1989: 223). In this

context what the editors of *Australian Feminism: A Companion* remarked seems pertinent "...not even attempt to impose a singular definition of feminism...because of the diversity in, and constant movement of, feminist terrain" (Caine et al., 1998: x). The editors of a journal called *Feminist Theory*, said in their first issue: "We neither wish to impose any form of theoretical orthodoxy nor any single definition of what counts as feminist theory" (Griffin et al., 2000: 5). The reluctance to define feminism can be seen in the compilers of feminist dictionaries too. As Maggie Humm, author of *The Dictionary of Feminist Theory*, said that it could only be "misleading to offer precise definitions of feminism because the process of defining is to enlarge, not to close down, linguistic alternatives; it is to evoke difference and to call up experience" (Humm 1989: xiv). Lastly, in her paper "Defining Feminism" Karen Offen, quoted one writer saying that "definition is a male prejudice" and that "the day we start defining feminism it's lost its vitality". However, Offen herself does not seem to concur with the idea, "As a practical matter, I find it difficult to accept the renunciation of definition that has recently become stylish in the wake of French feminist literary criticism (e.g. Alice Jardine, *Gynesis*). Knowledge is not well served by [refusing to define feminism].... The utility of definition depends on how it is done" (Offen 1988: 121 n4).

Thus, we see that feminism is too diverse to be restrained by a simple definition—as indicated by Tong's comment that its 'meanings are ever changing', or by the Oxford *Companion* editors' reference to the "diversity in, and constant movement of, feminist terrain"; and further, by Delmar's reference to the "fragmentation of contemporary feminism". The idea that feminism is diverse is usually seen these days by the use of the term 'feminisms' in the plural. Therefore, to define feminism would be to minify that diversity, as connoted by Jardine's comment that "dictionary meanings are suffocating", by Humm's comment that definition "closes down linguistic alternatives", and lastly, by the comment by the writer quoted by Offen to the effect that to define feminism would be to deprive it of its vitality. Besides, defining suggests something dictative, something doctrinaire and arbitrary—as pointed out by the

Feminist Theory editors' statement of their intention to avoid "imposing any form of theoretical orthodoxy", and Jardine's statement about "*demanding* a definition of what feminism is and, therefore, [demanding a definition] of what one must do, say, and be". It implies that defining feminism is a stratagem, a type of authoritarianism which directs are the do's and don'ts of feminism.

Although "Feminist thought resists categorization, especially categorization," writes Tong (1998) in her book *Feminist Thought,* yet the history of feminist thought has provided its own classifications like—liberal, radical, Marxist-socialist, which, "signal to the broader public that feminism is not a monolithic ideology, that all feminists do not think alike, and that, like all time-honored modes of thinking, feminist thought has a past as well as a present and a future" (Tong 1998: 1). In *Transforming Visions: Feminist Critiques in Communication Studies,* Sheryl Bowen and Nancy Wyatt pointed out that there was an apparent dearth of any proper definition of 'feminism' and 'feminist' because by nature these concepts seem to resist definitive statements (2). However, Bowen and Wyatt draw our attention to the simplified fact that feminism is concerned with women's lives; theories about humans; the nature of knowledge; the way in which knowledge is generated and legitimated; the "canon" of traditional knowledge; and process and connection (2-6).

In *Ain't I a Woman* (Hooks 1999: 195), Bell Hooks states, "Feminism is a commitment to eradicating the ideology of domination that permeates Western culture on various levels sex, race, and class, to name a few and a commitment to reorganizing US society, so that the self-development of people can take precedence over imperialism, economic expansion, and material desires." In *This Bridge Called My Back* (Smith 1981: 63), Barbara Smith remarks, "Feminism is the political theory and practice to free all women: women of color, working-class women, poor women, physically challenged women, lesbians, old women as well as white economically privileged heterosexual women. Anything less than this is not feminism, but merely female self-aggrandizement." Susan Faludi, remarks in *Backlash*

(Faludi 2006: 15), "Feminism asks the world to recognize at long last that women aren't decorative ornaments, worthy vessels, members of a special-interest group. They are half (in fact, now more than half) of the national population, and just as deserving of rights and opportunities, just as capable of participating in the worlds events, as the other half. Feminisms agenda is basic: It asks that women not be forced to choose between public justice and private happiness. It asks that women be free to define themselves instead of having their identity defined for them, time and again, by their culture and their men." Susan Douglas remarks poignantly in *Where the Girls Are* (Douglas 1995: 273), "Feminism is an ongoing project, a process, undertaken on a daily basis by millions of women of all ages, classes, ethnic and racial backgrounds, and sexual preferences. Feminism is constantly being reinvented, and reinvented through determination and compromise, so that women try, as best they can, to have love and support as well as power and autonomy."

Types of Feminism

Analyzing feminist theory and research as a scholarship field becomes easier by discussing the common, distinctive elements in the politics of doing research and scholarship that are shared by feminists. Karen Warren (1993) used the "boundaries of a quilt or collage" to describe what she calls *boundary conditions* of a feminist ethic. According to Warren, the boundaries "delimit the territory of the piece without dictating what the interior, the design, the actual pattern of the piece looks like. Because the actual design of the quilt emerges from the multiplicity of voices of women in a cross-cultural context, the design will change over time. It is not something static" (331). The feminist theory perspectives frequently used—the quilt designs we now often recognize—are briefly summarized here.

For example, *liberal feminism* is developed out of liberal political philosophy, arguing that through legal and political avenues of the mainstream, women can change laws and politics and therefore achieve gender justice. Throughout its history the liberal feminist movement has been and continues to be focused on eliminating female subordination, "…rooted in a set of customary and legal constraints blocking women's entrance to and success in the so-called public world" (Tong 1998: 2). Its long history is a testament to how well it has been able to adapt and change to the many issues confronting women. Liberal feminists focus on the centrality of an ideal state that respects all its citizens, thereby granting and protecting equal rights and equal opportunities for women and men. Here, the point is not to change but reform existing norms and systems so as to include women. Mary Wollstonecraft's *A Vindication of the Rights of Woman*, stressed on women's need to be educated just as well as men so that they can grow up to be moral and autonomous human beings (1975: 12-13). In the 19th century, John Stuart Mill and Harriet Taylor (Mill) wrote about women needing to be more involved in society and supported the suffrage movement. After several decades of struggle women were finally allowed to vote in 1920 when the 19th amendment passed. After the passage of the 19th amendment liberal feminism was quiet until the 1960s when it awoke during the civil rights movement by realizing that similar to race discrimination there was a great deal of sex discrimination inherent in the system. Betty Friedan's *The Feminine Mystique*, establishes her as a prominent feminist activist and an important leader in the liberal feminist movement. Liberal feminism has been criticized for focusing too much on women becoming like men, for emphasizing the rational above the emotional while humans need both and focusing on the individual and not on the community. However, with its focus on gender justice and its ability to adapt, liberal feminism is here to stay.

Marxist feminism focuses on class division as the major factor in women's oppression, paying attention to the intersections between women's work and women's self-perception. Marxist theory attempts to explain the structure of modern industrial society with special emphasis on class and labour. According to Marx, society is broken up into two classes containing those who own the means of production (factories, tools, capital) and the labourers who are exploited to produce the items demanded by the ruling classes (Tong 96). This exploitation is extended to women with the addition of sexism and gender inequality.

Marxist feminists are primarily concerned with the division of labour that keeps women in the domestic sphere and men in the workplace (Tong 110). In addition to this, when women do enter the workforce, they are delegated to jobs that are deemed appropriate for their gender and are usually underpaid for their work. For Marxist-feminist thought the focus is on the overhauling of capitalism and patriarchy as systems inherently exploitative and the change towards a different society.

Radical feminism describes women's oppression as being grounded in reproduction, mothering, gender, and sexuality. They call for women to absent themselves emotionally and sexually from men so they may realize their full and whole selves as women. In *Feminist Thought: A More Comprehensive Introduction*, Rosemarie Putnam Tong divides feminism into camps, the radical-libertarian feminists and the radical-cultural feminists, and then shows how two parties with the same basic theory and goal can have startling differences and multiple conflicts in pursuit of this goal. Whereas the radical-libertarian feminists wish to do away with the concept of femininity and its accompanying reproductive, mothering and sexual roles and aim for an androgynous society which combines both masculine and feminine characteristics for the individual as well as for society, the radical-cultural feminists, however, reject masculinity as a desirable quality and encourage women to embrace femaleness only. Women should emphasize traits culturally associated with women and de-emphasize traits culturally associated with men.

Psychoanalytic feminism theorizes that women's nature is not biologically determined, but socially constructed. Women's oppression is based on childhood experiences where masculinities and femininities are constructed and communicated, leading to the ways of thinking about oneself. Gender feminists stress that values traditionally associated with women are morally better values than those associated with men (Tong 1998: 131). These lines of thought emphasize the internal ways of thinking: for psychoanalytic feminism women must fight not only for their rights as citizens but also to free themselves from the "father within" and allow the space to think for themselves (Tong 1998: 171).

Cultural feminism proposes women should provide ways of being, thinking, and speaking that allow for openness, diversity, and difference.

Postmodern feminism focus on questions of meaning and identity, contending that these categories are fluid rather than fixed, and proposing that men and women may perform characteristics of either gender, or even slide between gender identities. Rosemarie Tong in *Feminist Thought* examines how the definitions and notions that were developed in France and became major modern definitions of women can be reconstructed and liberated to unshackle women from those definitions. This process is analysed in multiple ways which include existentialitical, psychoanalytical, and fictional literary viewpoints. According to Jacques Lacan, people internalize their roles, rituals and interrelated signs that regulate a society unconsciously, which is called "the Symbolic Order". Lacan insists it is the symbolic order that excludes women from a society.

Cyborg feminism has emerged as a way of theorizing women's relationship to science and technology. Specifically conceived by Donna Haraway, cyborg feminism has produced a major intervention in communication scholarship because it appropriates "androcentric" language to expose both bodies and science as socially constructed. Valuing hybridity, as she searches for ways to negotiate the difficulties posed by feminist research and women's political differences, Haraway declares: "Perhaps, ironically, we can learn from our fusions with animals and machines how not to be man, the embodiment of Western logos" (1991: 173). Postmodern feminists "take their intellectual cue from existentialist Simone de Beauvoir" (Tong 1998: 194) as they focus on women's "otherness" and Jacques Lacan, with their attention to the symbolic order of society and its internalization; and Jacques Derrida's deconstructionism that challenges "dualistic" thinking, speaking, and writing, and the artificial separation of body and mind, reason and emotion, self and other—as well as those between science and art or psychology and biology (Tong 1998: 195).

Contributions by women of colour have been influential, as they argue the condition of otherness enables woman to stand back and criticize the norms, values, and practices that the dominant culture seeks to impose on everyone. One such framework is *African feminism* (sometimes called *Womanism*) (Kolawole 1997; Oyewumi 2003), which foregrounds the diasporic experiences of women of African descent, finding links transnationally between Africa, the United States, the Caribbean, and Latin America. African and African-American women often find that they have more in common with men from their communities than with white American, Anglo, or European women and they sometimes organize around diasporic issues that would otherwise be overlooked such as forced marriage, female circumcision, or neo-colonialism (Guy-Sheftall 2006: 26).

In the search to "integrate viewpoints, improve inclusivity, and promote solidarity" is *ecofeminism*: "Ecofeminists claim that environmental issues are feminist issues because it is women and children who are the first to suffer the consequences of injustice and environmental destruction" (Gaard and Gruen 1993: 11). Gaard and Gruen also note that "ecofeminists believe that the current global crises are the result of the mutually reinforcing ideologies of racism, sexism, classism, imperialism, naturism, and speciesism" (25). Ecofeminist theory is theory in process, built on community-based knowing and valuing; the strength of this knowledge is dependent on the inclusivity, flexibility and reflexivity of the community in which it is generated. Further, ecofeminist theory grows out of dialogue and focuses on reaching consensus (32-33). Karen Warren (1993) wrote that ecofeminists insist that the sort of logic of domination used to justify the domination of humans by gender, racial or ethnic, or class status is also used to justify the domination of nature. Because eliminating logic of domination is part of a feminist critique—whether a critique of patriarchy, white supremacist culture, or imperialism—ecofeminists insist that naturism [discrimination against nature and other living organisms] is properly viewed as an integral part of any feminist solidarity movement to end sexist oppression and the logic of domination which conceptually grounds it (325-26). Rosemarie Tong's chapter on ecofeminism begins with a discussion of the close relationship between women and nature. She states that, in patriarchal culture, "women have been 'naturalized' and nature has been 'feminized'". Tong draws on the work of Karen Warren to solidify this assertion: "Warren emphasized that women are 'naturalized' when they are described in animal terms such as 'cows, foxes, chicks, serpents, bitches, beavers, old bats, cats, bird-brains, hare brains." Similarly, nature is "feminized when 'she' is raped, mastered, conquered... or when 'she' is venerated...as the grandest 'mother' of all." If this is true and emdash; that women and nature are symbolically interchangeable—it follows that what man does to nature, he may also do to woman. Francoise d'Eaubonne, an early ecofeminist, saw a direct link between the oppression of nature and the oppression of women. She claimed that the liberation of one could not occur without the liberation of the other. The ecology movement and the feminist movement are intertwined. This is the bedrock assumption of ecofeminism. Tong points out that ecofeminists are often likened to deep ecologists. Deep ecologists believe that nature has intrinsic value apart from human the values human place on it. It is human-centredness (anthrocentrism), deep ecologists feel that is at the root of the earth's degradation. Humans only care about the aspects of the earth that contribute directly to their own comfort and welfare. Eco-feminists differ, however, in that they feel that the problem is not human-centredness but rather male-centredness, or androcentrism.

Generally, ecofeminists seek to strengthen women's ties to nature rather than weaken them. They feel that women's physiological experiences lead to traits such as caring, nurturing, and intuitiveness and that these traits are undervalued in a male-dominated society. Tong states that they believe "traditional female virtues, not traditional male virtues, can foster improved social relations and less aggressive more sustainable ways of life". Mary Daly was a particularly fiery proponent of this belief feeling that men were death and destruction loving whereas women were life-giving and life-loving. According to Daly, nature is doomed unless women take action. Susan Griffin, another ecofeminist, asserted that humans needed to transcend the dualistic and linear thinking of patriarchy and embrace the passionate, subjective voice of female culture. Women, Griffins feels, need to speak up and integrate their unique perspective into the cultural dialogue. It is the only way to transcend the dualistic thinking that deems women and nature as inferiors.

Global feminism emerged out of international feminist movements and invoked the plural form to signal that these activists constantly strive for multiplicity of perspectives. The historical development of the feminist movement is also expressed and identified in "waves" which have prioritized specific social demands in different socio-economic historical periods.

A Historical Estimate

Although feminism seems to the modern reader, a phenomenon of the 20th century with the suffragettes of the 20s and the women's liberation movement of the 60s and 70s, it has always existed. It can even be traced back to Aristotle's declaration that, "The female is female by virtue of a certain lack of qualities," and St. Thomas Aquinas's belief that woman is an "imperfect man," and to texts going back as far as Aristophanes's comedy *Lysistrata*, "which is about how women achieved social change by withholding sexual favours from their men" (Ruthven 1984: 16). Sharon Spencer mentions Sappho of the 6th century BC as the greatest lyric poet of antiquity" and Christine de Pisan's work as the "first major work of feminist criticism" (Spencer 1982: 157). Pisan's *Epistre au dieu d'amours* (1399) was written against the biased representations of women in de Meun's work. In her *La cite des Dames* (1405), Pisan also argued that God created man and woman as equal beings. But it is Mary Wollstonecraft's *A Vindication of the Rights of Woman* (1792) which marks the first modern awareness of women's struggle for equal rights, and therefore it is the first milestone for the equality of the sexes. *A Vindication of the Rights of Woman* is one of the first works that can unambiguously be called feminist and which marks the first modern awareness of women's struggle for equal rights. Wollstonecraft saw that it was the education and upbringing of women that created their limited expectations based on a self-image dictated by the male gaze. Despite her perceived inconsistencies, reflective of problems that had no easy answers; this book remains a foundation stone of feminist thought (Walters 2005). K.K. Ruthven observes that "the analogy with slavery, which is present in Wollstonecraft's book, "becomes the dominant trope in nineteenth-century feminist writing, doubtless because of feminist involvement in the abolitionist movement" (Ruthven 1984: 29).

Seventy-seven years later, in *The Subjection of Women* (1869), John Stuart Mill expressed it very powerfully: "All men, except the most brutish, desire to have in the woman most nearly connected with them, not a forced slave but a willing one, not a slave merely, but a favourite. They have therefore put everything in practice to enslave their minds" (Mill 1974: 989-98). Sixty years later Virginia Woolf's *A Room of One's Own* (1929) developed and enhanced these views with a strong female sensibility and criticism. *A Room of One's Own* became an important precursor of feminist literary criticism. Here, Virginia Woolf argues that the male-dominated ideas of the patriarchal society prevented women from realising their creativity and true potential—In the first place, to have a room of her own, let alone a quiet room or a sound-proof room, was out of the question, unless her parents were exceptionally rich or very noble, even up to the beginning of the nineteenth century.... Such material difficulties were formidable; but much worse were the immaterial. The indifference of the world which Keats and Flaubert and other men of genius have found so hard to bear was in her case not indifference but hostility (Woolf 1981: 52).

In the book, *The Feminine Mystique*, Betty Friedan explored the roots of the change in women's roles from essential workforce during World War II to homebound housewife and mother after the war, and assessed the forces that drove this change in perception of women's roles. In her book, Friedan criticised "the dominant cultural image of the successful and happy American woman as a housewife and mother" (Leitch 1988: 308). According to Friedan, in the 1950s women had gone back to the house abandoning their jobs to men who came back from the war to claim their positions, and a feminine mystique was created in the media making the housewife and mother the ideal models for all women. Promoting women's ideal reality within the domestic realm, this mystique had reduced the identity of women to sexual and social passivity. Betty Friedan attempted to demystify this false feminine mystique, which she described as "a world confined to her own body and beauty, the charming of man, the bearing of babies, and the physical care and serving of husband, children and home" (Milllard 1989: 155) in order to renew the women's fight for equal rights. She had started a new consciousness—raising movement, and played a central role in developing the new discipline of women's studies.

Feminist writing in the early 1970s ranges from Gloria Steinem (*Ms.* magazine 1970), to Kate Millett's *Sexual Politics* (Millett 1970). Millett's uses her bleak survey of male writers and their attitudes and biases to demonstrate her thesis that sex is politics, and politics is power imbalance in relationships. Her pessimism is reflected in her description of "the desert we inhabit". From the same period come Shulamith Firestone's *The Dialectic of Sex*, Germaine Greer's *The Female Eunuch*, Sheila Rowbotham's *Women's Liberation and the New Politics* and Juliet Mitchell's *Woman's Estate*, the following year. Firestone based her concept of revolution on Marxism, referred to the "sex war," and interestingly, in view of the debates over patriarchy, claimed that male domination dated to "back beyond recorded history to the animal kingdom itself". Co-founder of *Redstockings* (Halbert 2004) Firestone, considered a radical, put "feminism" back in the vocabulary (Echolas 1989).

Thus, we can sum up the movement's history has gone through three waves, beginning in the 18th century.

Waves of Feminism

Although many people think of feminism as a singular school of thought that emerged fully formed in the 1970s, in fact there have been three successive "waves" of feminism in the United States, starting in the late 19th/early 20th centuries and continuing into the modern day. There are typically thought to be three waves of feminism, each of which concerned themselves with particular issues related to women. The feminist theory, its varied articulations and its ramifications in a literary context constitute a significant segment for critical endeavour. Feminist theory is a locale of writing which represents a critical and original contribution to current thinking and reveals the magnitude of women's individual and collective experiences and their struggles. It analyses how sexual divergence is constructed within any intellectual and common word and builds accounts of experiences from these differences. An elementary goal of feminist theory is to comprehend women's oppression in terms of race, sex, class and sexual preference and how to revolutionize it. Social theories, political movements, moral philosophies and literature, all of these have played a big role in spreading feminism across all sections of the society. But literature as a medium of expression has been most popular among the feminists largely because of its mass appeal. Feminist literatures, both fiction and non-fiction, have been rampantly written over the years to put forward the feminist ideals. Contemporary feminist writing deal with equal rights for women, domestic violence, sexual harassment of women, sexual objectification, patriarchal domination and all other forms of oppression that women of all societies have to suffer. The feminist movement has brought a sweeping variety of social and cultural change, its impact touching familial relations, religion, the place of women in society, gendered language, and relationships between men and women.

First Wave of Feminism

The "First Wave" of feminism began in the late 19th and early 20th century and focused mainly on opening up various opportunities for women, especially the right to vote (which had already been accorded to poor white and black men but had been regularly denied to women). Susan B. Anthony and Elizabeth Cady Stanton were two of the most important thinkers in this early stage of feminism. The key concerns of First Wave Feminists were education, employment, the marriage laws, and the plight of intelligent middle-class single woman. They were not primarily concerned with the problems of working-class women, nor did they necessarily see themselves as feminists in the modern sense (the term was not coined until 1895). First Wave Feminists largely responded to specific injustices they had themselves experienced. First Wave feminism was also frequently related to other social movements taking place at the time, including both the abolitionist and temperance movements, with many women urging politicians to vote for prohibition. During this time, the differences between men and women were an especial concern, and many feminists felt that, due to their moral superiority over men, women would bring much-needed purity to the world of politics.

Second Wave of Feminism

If, in simple terms, the first wave has demanded a civic, legal entity for women as proprietors and voters, with the suffragette movement, the second wave, working with and from the civil rights movement, has focused on expanding the agenda of legal recognition into women's equality in work, pay, welfare, control over one's body and access to child care and abortion, eradication of violence against women and generally extend full human rights for women (Dicker and Piepmeier 2003: 9). Some cultural critics (Walker 1992) observe that there was a major tidal shift when more voices by women of colour and global women began to be incorporated. The "Second Wave" of feminism is typically seen as starting in the 1960s and continuing into the 1990s and was particularly connected to other social movements occurring at the time such as the anti-Vietnam protests and the civil rights movement. Figures like Gloria Steinem and Betty Friedan are typically seen as the most prominent members of this wave of feminism. The Second Wave of feminism, although it did stress such important social and economic issues as equality in employment and sexual harassment, was also driven by other, more theoretical interests such as the differences between men and women and the political consequences of those differences. As in First Wave feminist thought, however, there was still a prevailing belief that men and women were essentially different, and that due to their nurturing and collaborative natures women would be able to bring about a peaceful world. The term 'Second Wave' was coined by Marsha Lear, and refers to the increase in feminist activity which occurred in America, Britain, and Europe from the late sixties onwards. In America, second wave feminism rose out of the Civil Rights and anti-war movements in which women, disillusioned with their second-class status even in the activist environment of student politics, began to band together to contend against discrimination. The tactics employed by Second Wave feminists varied from highly-published activism such as the protest against the Miss America beauty contest in 1968, to the establishment of small consciousness-raising groups. However, it was obvious early on that the movement was not a unified one, with differences emerging between black feminism, lesbian feminism, liberal feminism, and social feminism. Second Wave feminism in Britain was similarly multiple in focus, although it was based more strongly in working-class socialism, as demonstrated by the strike of women workers at the Ford car plant for equal pay in 1968. The slogan 'the personal is political' sums up the way in which Second Wave feminism did not just strive to extend the range of social opportunities open to women, but also, through intervention within the spheres of reproduction, sexuality and cultural representation, to change their domestic and private lives. Second Wave feminism did not just make an impact upon Western societies, but has also continued to inspire the struggle for women's rights across the world.

Third Wave of Feminism

When Rebecca Walker, daughter of author Alice Walker and Godchild of activist Gloria Steinem, published an article in *Ms.* entitled "I Am the Third Wave," it drew a surprising response. Young women from all over the country wrote letters informing the magazine of the activist work they were quietly engaged in and encouraging older feminists and leaders of the women's movement not to write them off. The front page of the Third Wave Foundation website explains that the organization strives to combat inequalities that [women] face as a result of [their] age, gender, race, sexual orientation, economic status or level of education. By empowering young women, Third Wave is building a lasting foundation for social activism around the country.

The current Third Wave highlights differences between and among women, often making visible the positive aspects of woman as "other". For example, with increasing globalization, women around the world have looked for ways to come together across national borders, mobilizing the universal category "woman" in order to fight for such common goals as human rights, poverty or illiteracy, while remaining loyal to locally specific struggles. "Third Wave" feminism, although it shares many of the interests of the first two waves (such as the empowerment of women), is also characterized by a desire of young women to find a voice of their own and to include various diverse groups in the fold of feminist thought. Rebecca Walker, who coined the term "Third Wave," is one of the most prominent figures in this wave of feminism.

This brief overview of the plurality of feminist theoretical frameworks demonstrates the complexity and sophistication of feminist thought, but also its flexibility and responsiveness to the real world of lived, material or other, experience. Readers will of course make up their own minds as to the most suitable analytical approach explored here, but it is important to recognize and respect the enormous contribution that each approach makes to our understanding of the human condition.

Feminism in the Indian Context

The contours of feminist thought and the feminist movements in the West have greatly influenced the women's movements in developing countries like India. The Western feminists and Western theoretical models of feminism have done a commendable job of deconstructing several age-old binaries that have characterised dominant philosophical and political thinking on gender. However, feminism, as it exists today in India has gone beyond its Western counterpart. As Uma Narayan rightly puts it, "Third World feminism is not a mindless mimicking of 'western agendas' in one clear and simple sense—Indian feminism is clearly a response to the issues specifically confronting many Indian women" (Weedon 1997: 13). Even, Maitrayee Chaudhuri in her collection *Feminism in India*, rejects claims that feminism in India has been a Western import (Bhasin and Khan 1986). Rather, she says, ideas about women's rights and gender construction have always been debated in India, but differently. Though there has been a great degree of variance in this theorising both historically and within different women's social movements today, one aspect that runs through all the work is the fact that feminism in

India has always had to negotiate around and distinguish itself from Western discourses. Kumari Jayawardena in her pioneer work on Feminist movements in Asia, in the late 19th and earth 20th century, defines Feminism as—"Embracing movements of equality within the current system and significant struggles, that have attempted to change the system" (Chaudhuri 2004).

In this definition, she considers these movements to be responsible for the formulation and consolidation of national identities which mobilized anti-imperialist movements during the independence struggle, and the remaking of pre-capitalist religion and feudal structures in attempts to 'Modernize' the Third World societies. The rich history of women's movements in India has been well documented by scholars. But it is almost impossible to separate "the history of action from the history of ideas". The first possible route of rethinking—what constitutes conceptual history?—Debates within women's organization in the colonial period about whether one ought or ought not to join the national movement, debates within the constituent assembly about the possible conflicts between the freedom of religion and freedom of women, debates between the left feminists and autonomous women's groups in the 1970s about the strategies and organizational structures; More debates were between the Dalit feminism and the mainstream feminism and between feminism and secularism, feminism and community identities—all these arise in the context of a history. Women studies and the women's movements in the post-1977 context have been closely intertwined. Until 1990s, Indians did not really have a body of feminists' scholars engaged in academic conversation within the corpus of what is Western-dominated international academic feminism.

Although feminism as an organized movement made its appearance in India late in the 1970s, it existed in spirit long before even the Western feminist movement had begun. As early as 15th century, Meera Bai and her struggle to remain faithful to her divine love is one of the early manifestations of feminist consciousness. Besides, in India's struggle for independence the women activists were also guided to a considerable extent by the feminist zeal. As Tharu and Lalita's landmark collection of women writings in India (1991) has shown, there was a prolific exchange of ideas about gender construction and gender norms well before the late 1800s when Tarabai Shinde is supposed to have written *A Comparison of Men and Women*. Seen as India's pioneering feminist literary critic, Shinde draws links between colonialism and the commodification of women's bodies. The Oxford-educated Parsi Christian reformer Cornelia Sorabji who saw education as the main means by which social transformation of women could be undertaken, Sorabji argued that it was not law but education that could be the panacea sought by reformers attempting to end the practice of child marriage. Rokeya Sakhawat Hossain's *Sultana's Dream* is a feminist utopia which envisions a world where women are in charge of the public sphere.

Feminism in Indian English fiction has a series of counters and ordeals on the part of woman to strike at the roots, to belong and assert her ideality in a transitional society. Like man, woman is born free, but she is in chains, not always and everywhere. All women do not conform, they rebel, they reconcile, and they are both Kali and Durga, symbols of destruction as well as creation. During the Vedic period, Indian woman enjoyed the pride of place with the extraordinary scholars like Gargi, Matreyi, Lopamudra, who walked equally with men. Even Sita, Savitri, Shakuntala and Draupadi, who make their appearance at a later period in history, were not said to be passive, submissive, docile and servile, Sita in the Ramayana has resisted the demoniac aggressiveness of Ravana, Shakuntala in the Mahabharata proved the strength of her nerves by meeting the challenge of Dushyanta, Draupadi displayed the female ferocity by washing her hair in the blood of Duhsasana who had attempted to disrobe her in the court of Kauravas. It is very rightly said, in the Indian context that, "Yatra Naryastu, Pujyante Ramanti Tatra Devataha" meaning, the gods reside in the place where woman is worshipped, woman is so indispensable to man's life, she is an adviser in his work, a slave in service to him, a partier in noble deeds, as earth in tolerance, a mother in affection, a harlot in bed and a friend in enjoyment:

"Karyeshu mantri,
Karaneshu dasi
Dharmeshu Patni,
kshamaya dharitri
sneheshu mata,
shayaneshu veshya
Range Sakhi Laxmana! Sakutome."

However, Manu's male-dominated code of conduct in *Manu Samhita*, stated that the woman in India lost her pedestal, and disappeared behind the *Pardah* during the Muslim rule. It was not before India's Independence movement, that Gandhi freed women from their subservient life, and engrossed them into the freedom movement; women broke their chains, walked hand in hand with men, raising their little fingers against the oppressive distatorial rule at home and abroad.

Feminism was theorized more differently in India than in the West. Feminist writings in India cannot be grouped into liberal, Marxist, socialist and black feminisms as the Western feminist theory categorises. Besides, unlike Western feminism, colonial essentialization of "Indian culture" and reconstruction of Indian womanhood as the epitome of that culture through social reform movements resulted in political theorization in the form of nationalism rather than as feminism alone. Historical circumstances and values in India make women's issues different from the Western feminist rhetoric. The idea of women as "powerful" is accommodated into patriarchal culture through religion. This has retained visibility in all sections of society; by providing women with traditional "cultural spaces". Another consideration is that whereas in the West the notion of "self" rests in competitive individualism where people are described as "born free yet everywhere in chains," by contrast in India the individual is usually considered to be just one part of the larger social collective, dependent for its survival upon cooperation and self-denial for the greater good. Besides, as opposed to the start of the Western feminist movement, India's feminist movement was spearheaded by men like—Dr. B.R. Ambedkar, Raja Ram Mohan Roy, Ishwar Chandra Vidyasagar, Keshav Chandra Sen, Malabari Phule, Gopal Ganesh Agarkar, Mahadev Govind Ranade, Dhondo and Keshav Karve.

Further, unlike the history of feminism in the West, the history of feminism in India is regarded as mainly a practical effort and mostly non-existent. The colonial venture into modernity brought concepts of democracy, equality and individual rights. The rise of the concept of nationalism and introspection of discriminatory practices brought about social reform movements related to caste and gender relations. The first phase of feminism in India was initiated by men to uproot the social evils of sati (widow immolation), to allow widow remarriage, to forbid child marriage, and to reduce illiteracy, as well as to regulate the age of consent and to ensure property rights through legal intervention. Women in this phase were categorized along with lower castes as subjects of social reforms and welfare instead of being recognized as autonomous agents of change. The emphasis was on recreating new space in pre-existing feminine roles of caring. The women involved were those related to male activists, elite, Western educated, upper caste Hindus.

Indian feminist scholars and activists have to fight to carve a different identity for feminism in India. They define feminism in time and space to in order to avoid the uncritically following Western ideas. Indian women negotiate survival through an array of oppressive patriarchal family structures: age, ordinal status, relationship to men through family of origin, marriage and procreation as well as patriarchal attributes—dowry, siring sons, etc.—kinship, caste, community, village, market and the state. It should however be noted that several communities in India such as the Nairs of Kerala, certain Maratha clans, and Bengali families exhibit matriarchal tendencies, with the head of the family being the oldest women rather than the oldest man. Sikh culture is also regarded as relatively gender-neutrals.

The diversity of Indian experience prove that there are multiple patriarchies and so also are there multiple feminisms.

Hence, feminism in India is not a singular theoretical orientation; it has changed over time in relation to historical and cultural realities, levels of consciousness, perceptions and actions of individual women and women as a group. The widely used definition is "An awareness of women's oppression and exploitation in society, at work and within the family, and conscious action by women and men to change this situation" (Bhasin and Khan 1986). Acknowledging sexism in daily life and attempting to challenge and eliminate it through deconstructing mutually exclusive notions of femininity and masculinity as biologically determined categories opens the way towards an equitable society for both men and women.

The problems and predicaments peculiar to the Indian women found artistic expression in the Indian literature in English since the 1970s. One of the major concerns of the contemporary literature all over the world has been to highlight the plight of women, their increasing problems, their physical, financial and emotional exploitation, and their mental anguish in the male-dominated society in every sphere of life. In almost all the countries, in the academic field, in woman forum, the main focus is to bring into light the oppression faced by women in various forms. The enforcement of the feminist movement, the establishment of various woman study centres and the formation of various welfare organizations are the indication of the fact that the voice of women is being heard. In order to reach the stage of being listened to, the woman writers had to struggle much and through their writing, they have been projecting their points, pleading, and rebel, often wished to be free and unrestrained. The article titled, "Redefining the F-word" published in *The Times of India*, special report, describes Indian Feminism in an interesting manner—"Regarded as a Western construct, feminism draws uncomfortable silence in India's living rooms. Yet, in a hundred different ways and across the country, whether spelt out as such or not, India's seen lots of feminist action. Only it's feminism, India-style. Never one concerted war, it's been more small battles, negotiated spaces and sacrifices. Scores of women-led struggles have been waged across the nation for long years. Feminism flourishes in a web of *mahila samitis* that dot the nation. Freedom to live and move in safety, equal access to health, education, jobs, credit, land rights and recognition as equal labour form their focus." "Feminism grew when more and more women became conscious of the impact of patriarchy. Initially influenced by the West, we realised that with India's cultural and traditional background, change won't be possible if you try to isolate the woman. "The fight for women's rights has to be one for community's rights," says feminist Jyotsna Chatterjee, of the Joint Women's Programme. Women in India are forever negotiating on their status. There's coming together on issues of home and security such as the Domestic Violence Act, and falling apart on issues such as the Uniform Civil Code or Women's Reservation Bill, where religious and community concerns hold precedence. "And why not?" says feminist Madhu Kishwar. "You fight for that part of your identity that is under threat. People follow diverse paths, parallel ways to fight. It's not sensible to put everybody into a single bracket as life situations vary greatly," she says.... Women's movements are not a post-Independence phenomenon either. Few have mapped the movement but *Feminism in India* (2005); edited by scholar Maitrayee Chaudhuri is seen as an anthology that "explores the infinite variety of Indian feminisms". Few beyond academia would know that the first Indian woman to write her autobiography was a Bengali housewife Rassundhara Devi in 1876, who taught herself to read and write in hiding, cites Samita Sen in a World Bank working paper, "Toward a Feminist Politics? The Indian Women's Movement in Historical Perspective". If in the late 19th century, women started questioning their subordination, early 20th century was time for action, finds Sen. Saraladevi Chaudhurani founded India's first women's group, Bharat Stree Mahamandal, in Allahabad in 1910. Several associations followed. The All India Women's Conference, launched in 1927, succeeded in ensuring an all-India presence. During the freedom struggle, "women used their traditional roles to mask a range of political activities such as hide weapons, shelter fugitives, provide cover to the men". Mahatma Gandhi catapulted them to the front, joining picketing lines and courting arrest. Interestingly, in 1931, Saraladevi, cites Sen, queried about the role women were playing: "The current Congress," said Saraladevi, "assigned to women the position of law-breakers only and not law-makers". In balancing nationalism with feminism, the latter took a backseat. As nationalistic fervour grew, the women's voice fell silent. Sen observes that with the new nation built on the promise of equal rights, the woman's question seemed settled. But soon enough, it was obvious that the reality was anything but that. Seldom is she looked at as a 'woman,' who if ensured the promised access to education, nutrition, and healthcare will figure out for herself the life she wants, points out activist Jacqueline de Chollet, who runs schools for girls in Rajasthan" (*Times of India*, 3 Jan. 2010).

Feminism, as a novel way of life, as a rising aspect, came into being in India with the feminine psyche attempting to redefine woman's role in the society. In their creative writings, the women writers like Kamala Markandaya, Kamala Das, Nayantara Sahgal, Anita Desai, Shashi Deshpande and others started discussing openly the sexual problems of women and questioning the gender-role expectations. The female protagonists in their writings evince sufficient vigour and courage to question the oppressive role of society, religion and culture, but yet they refrain from taking the paths suggested by the Western feminists. They rather seek to find their own paths.

Women writers in India are moving forward with their strong and sure strides, matching the pace of the world. We see them bursting out in full bloom spreading their own individual fragrances. They are recognized for their originality, versatility and the indigenous flavour of the soil that they bring to their work. Our women writers are writers first, I must insist. Gender is only incidental...but, one must admit, it does spice up their work. The image of women in fiction has undergone a change during the last four decades. Women writers have moved away from traditional portrayals of enduring, self-sacrificing women toward conflicted female characters searching for identity, no longer characterized and defined simply in terms of their victim status. In contrast to earlier novels, female characters from the 1980s onwards assert themselves and defy marriage and motherhood.

Recent writers depict both the diversity of women and the diversity within each woman, rather than limiting the lives of women to one ideal. The novels emerging in the twenty-first century furnish examples of a whole range of attitudes towards the imposition of tradition, some offering an analysis of the family structure and the caste system as the key elements of patriarchal social organization. They also re-interpret mythology by using new symbols and subverting the canonic versions. In conclusion, the work of Indian women writers is significant in making society aware of women's demands, and in providing a medium for self-expression and, thus, re-writing the History of India.

These women writers have given literary work in India an unmistakable edge. They are able to sensitively portray a world that has in it women rich in substance. Their women are real flesh-and-blood protagonists who make you look at them with awe with their relationships to their surroundings, their society, their men, their children, their families; their mental make-ups and themselves. One might tend to think of women writers only in a Mills and Boon context, but women writers in India have proved that they are made of sterner and more serious stuff than that. Our women writers have grappled with complex issues such as sensuality, servility, subjugation and society. They have handled them with a sense of balance, never disregarding our Indian traditions, yet discovering that there is more in the offing.

The image of the New Woman and her struggle for an identity of her own emerges in the Indian English novel. "Nayantara Sahgal," says Sinha, "is one such prominent Indian English novelist who has tried to depict women suffering due to sexist bias in patriarchal society and she envisions a world which should be based on equality and harmony between the two sexes" (Sinha 2008: 221-22). Such a struggle needs support structures outside the family to enable women to survive. Nayantara Sahgal uses this theme as the nucleus of *Rich Like Us* (1986). Other novels such as Rama Mehta's *Inside the Haveli* (1977), look more towards issues of traditional Indian culture, particularly the debate on female education. Another example of the Western-educated female protagonist's quest for her cultural roots is Githa Hariharan's *The Thousand Faces of Night* (1992). As a writer primarily committed to feminist and social issues, Hariharan stated: "My work grows out of my feminism and other political beliefs" (Hariharan Sept. 2005). "Anita Desai's fictional oeuvre," says Dr. Sinha, "has undoubtedly carved her a distinct niche in the contemporary fictional world. What makes her remarkable is her attempt to shift the focus from socio-political realities as is evident in the novels of Kamala Markandaya, Ruth Prawer Jhabvala and Nayantara Saghal to the exploration of the inner reality—the unexplored realm of the female psyche, the poignant evocation of human predicament and the sensitive apprehension of the existentialist vision of anguish, abandonment and despair" (Sinha 2008: 206). Her novels have Indians as central characters, and she alternates between female-centred and male-centred narrative. Her later novels, written since she moved to the USA, reveal all the characteristics of diasporic fiction, that is, a concern with the fate of immigrants, and a growing distance from the reality of India, which is viewed from the outside. Manju Kapur's fiction stresses on the woman's need for self-fulfillment autonomy, self-realisation, independence individuality and self-actualization. "I am interested," says Kapur, "in the lives of women, whether in the political arena or in domestic spaces. One of the main preoccupations in all my books is how women manage to negotiate both inner and outer spaces in their lives—what sacrifices do they have to make in order to keep the home fires burning and at what cost to their personal lives do they find some kind of fulfillment outside the home" (Kapur 7 June 2006).

PERSPECTIVES ON FEMININITY AND MASCULINITY IN SHASHI DESHPANDE'S *THAT LONG SILENCE*

Masculinity is a way to explain and describe the broad spectrum of realities associated with men and their worldview. "Masculinity", remarked Connell, "is not a static phenomenon based on the universally common structure of patriarchy; instead it is dynamic phenomenon which takes different shapes and forms, which vary within and across time, space and cultures" (Connell 1995). Masculinity has been, usually, defined as a way to describe man, manliness, being vigorous, being active, having qualities considered approximate to a true man. However, masculinity has been redefined as "different ideologies among different culture and social groups" (Leavant and Santra 1999) and "masculinity as being central to male gender roles linked to beliefs about the essentiality of men adhering to culturally defined standards for male behaviours" (Pleck 1995). The hegemonic nature of masculinity (Connell 1987) places it over various subordinated masculinities as well as over women in a socio-political hierarchy based on power and control.

Though various dimensions of masculinity across the world have been explored, studies on 'masculinity' are scarcely done or are being done in Indian context. In this context, Avanish Kumar rightly asserts, "India, as secular democratic country, although, developing towards the goals of making a free, just and equitable society, free of all the discrimination based on cast, creed and religion, as enumerated in Indian constitution, is still a country where gendered masculinities and patriarchal values stand as a main barrier in addressing the range of social and developmental issues and realigning millennium development goals. Various forms of gender based violence, marginalisation of women in mainstream development initiatives, poor health, education status and high rate of mother's mortality, along with traditional gendered discriminations necessitate an urgent attention to the issue of engendering the development process and society, through 'gender mainstreaming', 'redistribution of reproductive roles among genders' and making 'men as partners' in the empowerment of women" (www.insightresearchnetwork.org).

The ancient gender equation spoke of unchallenged male supremacy and female subjugation. Modern times have upset this unbalanced gender equation with more and more woman being emancipated through education and careers. In this changing scenario, it is natural that the mindset of the male also transforms into a tolerant and inclusive one giving space for women to find their own strength. The Indian male is caught in the midst of a rapidly changing social setup with empowered women vying for space in his professional and personal arena and one is left wondering if masculinity is in crisis? Thus, we see that masculinity cannot be understood in isolation but in relation to the feminine as one construct cannot exist without the other. The relationship between the two sexes has been, over the ages, one of power struggle and it is more so in Modern India where women are assertive, educated and self-reliant to some extent. In this scenario, men has to redraw the boundaries to establish his superiority even within marital relationship. To show the changing equation between men and women, I would focus in this essay, on Shashi Deshpande's novel, *That Long Silence.*

Shashi Deshpande sees herself as a fiction writer concentrating on the women's world and its problems. She rises from the narrow confines of feminist problems and constantly explores the need for human relation and interdependence. In her fiction it is never a question of man or woman but man and woman. Her characters' struggles are those of ordinary women fighting to be themselves rather than conform to stereotypes—to a fixed idea of how women should be. Deshpande does not want to see her novel only within the framework of feminist concerns; they are novels like any other with a gamut of issues and experiences. As she remarks—"I always feel kind of wronged when people say I write about women's problems, because I always feel I write about human beings, many of whom happen to be women. But then when I look back at my work and I think about what issue has mattered most, it is the conflict between the idea women have of themselves and the idea that society imposes on them of what being a woman is. And there's a struggle to conform to this image, the guilt when you can't do that. I think this image, especially in India, comes through religion, through myth, through literature, through cultural stereotypes, through movies, they're all very strong. So I've been discarding all those stereotypes and all the mythical images" [http://www.bbc.co.uk/worldservice/arts/features/womenwriters/deshpande_work.shtml]. Drawing its title from a 1907 "British Feminist Manifesto" it employs a first person confessional mode, with its setting entirely domestic and its action almost entirely in the realm of the protagonist's conspicuousness. As the novel centres around the protagonist Jaya's mental and emotional journey, it has been tagged as a 'feminist novel'. When Shashi Deshpande wrote the novel *That Long Silence*, she had no intention of writing a feminist tract, but as the novel appeared to be gender specific in the narration of the story of Jaya, a woman who found herself questioning her life, her beliefs and her relationships with others, it has been called a feminist text. The title of *That Long Silence* is taken from the pronouncement of Elizabeth Robins: "If I were a man who cared for the world I lived in, I almost think it would make me a shade uneasy—the weight of the long silence of one half of the world." [Robins, Elizabeth. A Speech in WWSL, 1907. Quoted by Shashi Deshpande in 'Epigraph', *That Long Silence* (New Delhi: Penguin, 1989).]

That Long Silence, by Deshpande revolves around Jaya and Mohan, who belong to a middle-class Indian Brahmin family. Mohan is involved in a swindle and hence he has to move away from his house to a temporary residence till the case is resolved. The family has to comply since he takes decisions without consulting his wife or anybody else in the family. He exercises hegemonic masculinity. The hegemonic image of manhood is constructed through differences with a variety of 'others'—racial or sexual minorities and women. The hegemonic definition of masculinity is "constructed in relation to various subordinated masculinities as well as in relation to women", writes sociologist Connell (183). Mohan takes Jaya for granted. Though Jaya does not want shift, she is forced. She says: "I remember now that he had assumed I would accompany him, had taken for granted my acquiescence in his plans. So had I. Sita following her husband into exile, Savitri dogging Death to reclaim her husband, Draupadi stoically sharing her husband's travails... (*That Long Silence* 11).

The novel offers a sensitive and realistic dramatization of the married life of Jaya and her husband Mohan, questioning the very institution of marriage. It revolves around the inner perception of the protagonist, a woman who is subtly drawn from inside, a woman who "finds her normal routine so disrupted that for the first time she can look at her life and attempt to decide who she really is" (King, 1988). But could she? The question that keeps haunting her is "who am I?" (24). She fails to find herself. She is "an utter stranger, a person so alien that even the faintest understanding of the motives of her actions seemed impossible" (69). Hence her agonized cries—"I can't hope, I can't manage. I can't go on" (70). In such a stifling domestic set up she finds her female identity effaced. Her dilemma is beautifully expressed in these lines: "I could and couldn't do all the things that were womanly and unwomanly..." (83). Jaya is Suhasini and also Seeta, the pseudonym she assumes to write columns about the plight of the middle class housewife. Both Suhasini and Seeta are as Jaya says—"the many selves waiting to be discovered...each self-attached like a Siamese twin to a self of another person, neither able to exist without the other" (69). Deshpande's novels sympathetically record the lives of such women as one of her themes. She has endeavoured to transmit the basic anxiety, loneliness and helplessness of their situation. The novel sensitively presents how a woman's existence is confined within domesticity and how all forms of oppression perpetuated on her are convincingly rationalized generating a closed-mind syndrome. The figure of Mohan's mother can be quoted as an example. In Jaya's narration, "the woman's crouching in front of the dying fire, sitting blank and motionless, the huddled bundles of sleeping children on the floor, the utter silence" (35).

The novel is described in flashbacks. The crux of the story is Mohan's malpractice in his office at the instigation of Mr. Agarwal, in the matters of contracts, tenders and commissions. Agarwal is an expert in these matters were as Mohan is an amateur, when Mohan denies a ministers' relative's favour/ demand, the whole mess is dug-up, with enquiry, scandal and final disgrace. At this point Agarwal advises Mohan to hide for some time and to quit the Churchgate posh house till the storm blows over. So Jaya and Mohan move into the Dadar flat of Jaya's maternal uncle Makarandamma, who had given this house to Jaya. The children go out for a holiday. When Mohan is facing an inquiry he loses his well-paid job, which was, in other words, 'terrible security'. This reminds us of the army wives, who were reduced to destitution on their husbands being thrown out of jobs and arrested later. But in the Indian context, it is necessary to understand, why Mohan chose corrupt means of money making? Sudhir Kakar views that—Super-ego, the moral agency is weakly differentiated and insufficiently idealized in Indians. But in the west, an individual's behaviour is constantly regulated by the proscriptions of the Super-ego, in a Hindu it is "Communal conscience" that regulates—meaning that communal conscience comprises family and Jati norms, it is a social man's individual format. For an Indian, there are many external 'watchmen' to patrol his activities, relationships especially in all social hierarchies. It is this importance of relationships that rules the life of an average Indian, rather than the importance of healthy social values.

Mohan is not an exception here; he has been an obedient, dutiful son. Inspite of the inhuman treatment meted out to him by his father and by extension he is a dutiful husband; He helps his family financially and attends the death anniversary of his father every year, and bears the total expenditure of the ceremony. As a junior engineer in Lohanagar, he make's himself a scapegoat in the corrupt deals of the chief engineer for the want of spacious living quarter for his family. In Bombay under the influence of his friend Mr. Agarwal, he accepts illegal gratification to provide a comfortable life for his family and so that his children might attend a good school. He says, "It was for you and the children that I did this, I wanted you to have a good life. I wanted the children to have all those things I never had" (19). For the first time, in her married life Jaya feels a strong, strange emotion of anger at this unjustified accusation made by Mohan. This accusation further leads to a re-assessment, self-interrogation of seventeen long years of their married life in the mind of Jaya. She too had nurtured a beautiful dream—vision of married family life, as seen in advertisement—"Those cozy, smiling, happy families in their gleaming homes spelt sheer poetry to me" (3). She had even accepted Mohan's version of themselves without a murmur—"...People in secure job, cushioned by insurance and provident funds with two healthy, well fed children going to good schools" (5).

Jaya's self-interrogation brings forth the truth that—traditionally, a woman has an identity only as a "husband's wife or father's daughters or son's mother". The real face, the real identity never comes out. It is like trying to look to know how really one looks like. Ten different mirrors show ten different faces. The personality of Jaya is not traceable for she is defined only in relation to others. The novelist being aware of the constraints present in the Indian society defines freedom of Indian women from the point of view of the Indian socio-cultural milieu. The attitudinal difference between Jaya and Mohan brings in a matching silence. She only babbles replies to all his questions. She decides to be silent. It is only towards the fag end of the novel, she decides to break her long silence—the author very wisely keeps the areas of consequences, "What if she actually breaks the silence." The end, thus is left to the imagination of its reader. Jaya's silence, its apprehensions are rooted in every woman's soul in a different form. Generally a woman's silence is often understood as her symbol of contentment, toughness.

But through the stream of consciousness technique, the novelist, makes it quite clear that even in the educated upper middle classes, the inherent value of intelligent and capable woman is affected by her social and married status, for the society treats her as an object or as a possession but never as an individual. She being a woman, Jaya is forced to accept the social and familial responsibilities. Mohan's misfortunes, his accusation turns out to be Jaya's traumatic experience. A sense of insecurity is the natural feeling when Mohan's job is at risk, which gets doubled with her son Rahul's disappearance from their family friends—Rupa and Ashoka—who had taken their children on a holiday tour, comes as a bolt from the blue. This is, in reality an additional despair, her carefully built sparrow-house seems to be cracked and exposes the inside very cruelly. "It was like a house collapse during the monsoon. There was something desolating about the ease with which what had seemed so substantial fell away, almost contemptuously, leaving behind an embarrassing nakedness" (174).

This truth has a striking effect on her. Earlier she has been expecting something awful/woeful to befall on her and mentally she welcomes it. She had thought of many options for dealing with the crisis, like a rational individual, such as suicide—an imaginative poetic death "The four of us walking peacefully into the sea in the mellow light of the setting sun" (10).

Mohan had renamed, Jaya at the time of marriage as "Suhasini," meaning "a soft, smiling, placid, motherly woman" (15-16). Ever since she was named as Suhasini she felt that her identity was in a dilemma and she feels disoriented. On her secret visit to her posh Churchgate home she sees her divided self clearly—"And now nothing seemed to connect me to this place, nothing bridged the chasm between this prowling woman and the woman who had lived here. I was conscious of a faint chagrin at her disappearance. Wasn't it I who had painfully laboriously created her? Perhaps, for that very reason, she could not evade me entirely" (168). In keeping with the traditional concept of docile wives, and silent woman, Ajji remarks—"Look at you—for everything a question, for everything a retort. What husband can be comfortable with that?" (27). Women are the unquestioning victims of generation of conditioning in which a girl/woman is unchangeably slotted.

Mohan is so firm in his rights that he demands, and his wife silently accepts the absolute authority of patriarchy, which is vividly narrated by Mohan to Jaya—"I can—see a picture of extraordinary clarity and vividness—the woman (Mohan's mother) crouching in front of the dying fire sitting blank and motionless, the huddled bundles of sleeping children (Mohan, his brothers and sisters) on the floor, the utter silence, the loud knock at the door.... They had all had their food, except her. Though she always waited for him, their father, however late he was (and he never gave her any indication of when he would be back) she had asserted herself in this that she would not make the children wait for him. She gave them their dinner, even the older ones and then she cooked rice for him again for he would not, and he made it clear to her, what he called food as, "your children's disgusting leavings". He wanted his rice fresh and hot, from a vessel that was untouched. She had just finished cooking this second cooking and was waiting, hoping, perhaps that he would not be too late, for it wouldn't do to let the food get cold and as for lighting the fire again, that was unthinkable" (15-16). At last, when he came in, he went straight to the bathroom to wash. By the time he returned, she had his plate ready. Hanging his shirt on a peg on the wall, he sat down, drank a glass of water, poured some water into his palm to sprinkle ritually around his plate and then he paused. "Why is there no fresh chutney today?" he asked, not looking at her. She mumbled something. The next second, he picked up his heavy brass plate and threw it, not at her, but deliberately on the wall, which it hit with a dull clang. He wore his shirt and went out of the house. This is silently watched by the children, the mother silently picks up the plate, cleans the floor and the wall of all the splattered food, and wipes it, she once again cooks rice and prepares fresh chutney, and sits down to wait, when her children, who had woken up by the clanging sound of the plate, finally drift off to sleep again—"She was still sitting there in front of the fire, silent, motionless" (36). Mohan's reaction after this narration is quite revealing. "God.... She was tough. Women in those days were tough" (36).

But Jaya discerns the unlimited despair in the heart of the 'wounded women,' she went on working for the man who wounded her. Her struggle continuous, her weapons are 'silence and surrender'. What hurt the sensitive readers is not only the cruelty of a husband, but also the insensitivity of a son, which displays the continued discrimination against women. Her son Mohan, who has been a witness, to this incident, never condemned his father. He eulogizes (recognizes) his mother, the virtuous women, "instead—She was tough, Women in those days were tough" (36).

Consequently, her husband loses his status, and she her identity, her selfhood. She comes to realize that—"The real picture, the real 'you' never emerges. Looking for it is as bewildering as trying to know how you really look. Ten different mirrors show you ten different faces" (1). The protagonist Jaya realizes that in order to attain self-hood, a woman must transcend silence, negation and self-alienation. A woman's relation with her family must burgeon within the totality of her life as a woman, only then it can lead to a harmonious fulfillment.

Thus, it becomes evident that Jaya is a fragmented self with a tormented consciousness. Evidently, she does not know her identity and does not enjoy individuality of her own. She sees herself as someone's daughter, wife and mother, having no status of her own. She therefore says: "I was born. My father died when I was fifteen. I got married to Mohan. I have two children and I did not let a third live" (2). Leading the life of 'a pair of bullocks yoked together,' Jaya's married life becomes unbearable and monotonous for her—"Worse than anything else had been the boredom of the unchanging pattern, the unending monotony" (4).

Jaya also finds herself in the midst of a domestic tension when she tries to know about her husband's (Mohan's) corrupt practices at office. In order to avoid exposure in public, Mohan shifts from his posh Church gate flat to a small apartment at Dadar, where they had once lived soon after their marriage. Here the couple sink into utter silence in a mood of frustration and depression, without sharing their ideas. Jaya is terribly disturbed by the prevailing circumstances in the family and she starts questioning herself.

Shashi Deshpande gives perfect examples of women who submitted always to insults, injuries and humiliations—with tremendous patience without any complaint. Kusum is an adopted girl by the childless Vanita Mami—who passively surrenders to the insecurity which pursues not only in her mother's home but also in her new house after marriage. Kusum's madness and accidental death her jumping into a dry well, represent those women 'who succumb before submission. Vanita Mami,' "who had never known, what it was to choose" (45) is another face, traditionally a suppressed woman. Her mother-in-law ruled her after the marriage and hence she had a passive life and had no role to play in decision-making—Jaya recalls, "Since the day she got married she, like the rest of Ai's family, was dominated and ruled by that ghoul, her mother-in-law my other—Aji. Even Vanita Mami's saris were chosen for her by the old woman. Later there was Ai, who went back to her old home after Appa's death; there still is Ai" (45).

It is this Vanita Mami who advises Jaya to please her husband even to the extent of accepting the existence of his mistress Saptagiri. Aji also reinforces the traditional concept of docile wives and silent women as the rules and regulations of traditional Indian marriages were heavy. The wife was forced to subordinate her own needs to those of her family, and to bear the exploitation and suffering with willingness. Any resistance to its androcentric rules is again considered to be the western influence of decadence. Even today, we strongly cling to the various forms of female oppression, exalting and glorifying them with the proactive norms of our life. The continued exaltation of self-effacing norms creates an environment which pressurizes a woman to accept or at least not to resist them. Often silence is the only option to a woman in such situations.

They suffer and die without uttering a single word in protest. Mohan's sister, Vimala dies in silent agony without getting any help from her in-laws, reliving her mother's fate. Her mother's photograph reminded Jaya of "floury hands dealing out a macabre punishment to her face" (38). Jaya could see the red bruise clearly seen on the white clown's mask. Vimala wanted and claimed to be different from her mother, but their suffering binds them together in a common fate. Jaya realizes it when she remarks, "Yet I can see something in common between them, something that links the destinies of the two—the silence in which they died" (39).

Jaya is quite a different personality when compared with Mohan's mother and sister, who within their duties, responsibilities and freedom excelled without a murmur. But, when Jaya tries to set up herself in those defined roles, the innate assertive traces inculcated in her by her father surfaces several times in her married life. On the contrary, Mohan's mother's married life was spent in utter suffering due to her husband's callousness. When she died with a huge round Kumkum on her forehead—"blessed woman who died as a Sumangali, with her husband yet living," (38) she was considered to be a very fortunate woman. His sister Vimala suffered in silence, her haemorrhage followed the footsteps of her mother, and "she sank into a coma and died a week later, her silence intact" (39). Her silence was very well appreciated and was given a loud applause. Jaya, too tries, her level best to imbibe the tradition of silence of her mother-in-law and sister-in-law, by enacting the role of a devoted wife and dutiful mother, but the role playing is not as natural as it should have been the cracks are soon visible. Once, she could not control her anger, she retorts back at Mohan, paying back his anger in the same measure—"Then, getting the feel of it, I had met his anger with my own, deliberately using it as a weapon, raging, furious—I had flung accusations, wildly at him" (81).

The other women characters in the novel Jeeja—Jaya's servant and her distant cousin Kusum hadn't experienced silence. Kusum had articulated her opinion, desire, and feelings even before her marriage. But even after marriage when she had to internalize all her pain and anger, she becomes insane. She becomes a burden to herself and to others, including her children.

At last, she killed herself. Silence, in a way becomes a symbol of high endurance on the part of a person who is silent. May be the genes are carried and are seen in the grandchildren's behaviour. Rahul, Jaya's son, is silent from the beginning, she is really worried about his silence throughout the day. "The last few months there had been silence in his room, it had frightened me" (49). He had not done well in his exams and had a very bad result. Mohan was angry but Rahul was silent. Jaya remarks—"It had made me uneasy that Rahul had listened silently, denying nothing, not excusing himself" (49). But somehow his silence broke "into open revolt," (49) when his father tried to impose his practical advice on him. He did it so soon and so easily because he was boy. But a girl could not have revolted thus, because the teaching given to her in an Indian society enforced silence. "Her Ajji, along with silence had taught her to 'wait' the waiting game" (30). For a man waiting brings in restlessness but for woman the game of waiting starts quite early in her childhood—"wait until you get married, wait until your husband comes, wait until you go to your in-law's home, wait until you have kids. Yes, ever since I got married I had done nothing but wait" (30).

Jaya by nature has inherited tenderness, she relents for she cannot see Mohan shattered, yet her entire pent up anger surfaces when Mohan's professional life faces crisis, and the blame is showered on Jaya and children. She now realize that the seventeen long years of her married life had failed to make them one emotionally and intellectually, only their physical bodies had occasionally met, not their souls, "We were two persons, A man, A woman" (8).

Shashi Deshpande opposes the patriarchal establishments which unnerve and cripple the innate creativity, individuality of Women. Her heroines get married with a rosy dream and hope of getting respect, security and status in the society, but they are utterly disappointed and disillusioned. In exploring and transcending the boundaries of the female gender, Deshpande creates initial revolters, but finally they compromise. Jaya is such a character who experiences the gravitational pull of patriarchy and tradition. Her absorption into the family fold and tradition is so total that from a fiercely independent girl, she gradually deteriorates into a "stereotype of a woman, nervous, incompetent, always in need of help, wanting to build an edifice of security around her husband and children, believing it to be a burrow into which she can crawl like a reptile and feel safe" (148). Deshpande concretizes Jaya's anxiety in the well-known childhood bed-time story of the wise sparrow, who built a home of wax and the foolish crow, who built her house of dung. On a rainy night the crow's house collapses forcing her to seek shelter at the sparrows. The sparrow is so possessive of her house and attached to the safety and welfare of her family members, that, she keeps the crow waiting out in the rain, for a considerable time. She allows the crow in her home only when the crow is thoroughly drenched and then guides it to the hot pan to warm itself. The foolish crow hops on to the hot pan and gets burnt to death. Jaya's married life has been lived on the same lines as that of the sparrow. Attending to the needs of the husband and tending and caring of the children becomes her full-time occupations she recalls in unequivocal terms that, "Mohan is her profession, career and means of livelihood" (75).

She follows her aunt's advice unconsciously and treats her husband as a "sheltering tree" (32). "She, like Gandhari of the Mahabharata symbolically bandages her eyes and grows blind to his weakness. Like Sita, who followed her husband into exile, she follows Mohan into the concrete jungle-Bombay" (11).

Significantly the column she maintains is entitled 'Seeta'. Incidentally, the novel is a critical analysis of one of our social institutions—Marriage. The moral of the story of the foolish crow and that of a shrewd sparrow, she learns is to "stay at home, look after your babies, keep out the rest of the world, and you are safe" (17). Thus marriage means—to be at home, to take care of the children and the husband and to be away from the rest of the world. In a way, marriage hinders the growth and right to free expression of a wife and a mother. The society is made to believe in labelling all the relationships a (married) woman has. A woman's contribution to the society is in terms of her role as an obedient wife, daughter and sister. The very thoughts of the collapse of her marriage, particularly those fears relating to the possibility of Mohan's death, keep constantly haunting her; "I had lived in constant panic that he would die, I had clung at him at night, feeling with relief the warmth of his body, stroking his chest letting my palms move with his even deep breaths. The thought of living without him had twisted my insides. His death had seemed to me the final catastrophe. The very idea of his dying had made me feel so bereft that tears had flowed effortlessly down my cheeks. If he had been a little late coming home, I had been sure he was dead. By time he returned, I had, in my imagination shaped my life to a desolate widowhood" (96-97).

In this small apartment in Dadar, Mohan and Jaya due to frustration and depressions sink into silence without talking and sharing their ideas. Jaya, who is terribly, disturbed starts interrogating herself and she realizes her situation as—"The real picture, the real 'you' never emerges. Looking for, it is as bewildering as trying to know how you really look. Ten different mirrors show you ten different faces" (1).

She is a fragmented self with a continuous tormented consciousness; she cannot recognize her identity and does not enjoy her own individuality. She only sees herself as some one's daughter, wife and mother, devoid of her own identity. Moreover, she in her depths of unconsciousness, is quite apprehensive of the disasters that take place in her life in the shape of a serious threat to her much prized and carefully built marriage and its temple—home.

The novel has three distinct phases of feminism. In the first place/phase it is seen as the imitation of role models whereas the heroine has crossed the limits—imitation leading to anger and protests of all kind. The major concern and thrust of the novel is the second phase of feminism in Jaya's life—whenever she looks back in her life, it is a scene of no sense of nostalgia or yearning, it is merely a feeling of suppressed anger, resentment. In course of seeking shelter during her traumatic situation in her neurotic state evades her personality as an adult. Her suffering initiates the process of self-discovery in her, leading in the final analysis to accept the fresh perception of life. In a way her suffering has a beneficial effect on her personality. It further strengthens her to emerge with certain willingness to compromise with life and its problems. Thus, in order to achieve a state of complete family life, as a woman, Jaya is forced to suppress every aspect of her wants, needs, desires that simply refused to fit into her role-model of a wife and a mother. Her other two most important aspects are firstly, her writing career and secondly, her association with Kamat. This relation of hers with Kamat needs a clear understanding at the outset. Kamat's role in the novel is a shadowy one. Basically he is an advertiser and lives alone in the apartment above the Kulkarnies at Dadar—Bombay. He is somehow different from other men, for he has no reservations against doing "unmanly" things like—Cooking, washing, etc. He is a smooth, floating personality, sympathetic, objective in approach, listens very attentively to all the womanly talks, carries himself with ease and grace in the company of women. Jaya is more attached to Kamat—but this can be termed only as a platonic affair, for it is short of a full-fledged affair. Kamat's one quality of treating woman as an equal endears Jaya to the maximum extent, only because she has seen men wearing different faces, with a false smile, but Kamat brings Jaya into herself—"It had been a revelation to me that two people, a man and a woman, could talk this way. With this man, I had not been a woman. I had been just myself—Jaya" (153).

Mohan and Jaya had 'so asexual' a relationship that she has never known how to address her husband. But it is in Kamat's presence that she becomes uninhibited and sheds all the crippling silence she had imposed on herself, erasing every public sign of her identity. It is from Kamat, once again, she gets the best of her father's concern for her re-assurances and comfort and the attention that she would like to have from Mohan. Kamat dares enough to chide her like her father, whenever, she is in the wrong—"I am warning you—beware of this 'women are the victims'—theory of yours. It'll drag you down into a soft, squishy bog of self-pity. Take yourself seriously, woman. Don't sulk behind a false name" (148). He supports and encourages her like an elder brother, "Spew out your anger in your writing, women, spew it out," (147) and at the same time, he pays beautiful compliments like an ardent lover—"Your name is like your face" (152). His absolute nature makes Jaya confide in him things she would never dare mention to Mohan. When one of her stories (which she wrote under the pseudonym name Seeta) is rejected by many writers, she turns to Kamat for solace. When she feels particularly sad about her father Appa's death, she involuntarily finds herself in the comforting embrace of Kamat. It becomes difficult for her to distinguish between him and Appa for a second. But her body responds to his gentle look, voice and touch and momentarily her ego and id clash with the ferocity of two fighters. She remembers that experience—"There had been nothing but an overwhelming urge to respond to him with my body, the equally overwhelming certainty of my mind that, I could not do so. Later, there had been confusion" (157).

Very quickly she overcomes and rejects the instinctual urge—it is not in the interest or sentiment of safeguarding her marital bliss.

In order to overcome this apprehensive urge towards Kamat, that night, she deliberately arouses desire in Mohan and makes fierce love to him. In her case and in many cases of other, she reasons the man-woman relation especially within the limits of marriage, is dictation by treachery, deceit, betrayal. In order to maintain her marital citadel, Jaya's gives up her writing career and Kamat. Very systematically she alienates herself from everything and everybody that posed even the remotest threat to the peace of her family. Jaya fails to identify herself and doesn't enjoy her own individuality. She sees herself as some one's daughter, wife and mother, shunning her own identity, she therefore remarks—"I was born. My father died when I was fifteen. I got married to Mohan. I have two children and I did not let a third live" (2). This last sentence directly hints at an abortion of her third child without her husband's knowledge. The word abortion is another name or face of infanticide, and shows the unethical practice of a wife. Till now, she has led a passive role-model life to fit her husband's requirement. She even lives up to this dedicated wife's role at the cost of losing her own identity. She remembers her relationship with her husband —"I am Mohan's wife I had thought, and cut off the bits of me that had refused to be Mohan's wife" (191). She feels at this point that her married life has turned out to be unbearable, monotonous and moving in a fixed portrait pattern, "worse than anything else had been the boredom of the unchanging pattern, the unchanging monotony" (4).

Both of them are leading their life like "a pair of bullocks yoked together". The one was pretending, as most couples do, to be happy. But in reality, in a real happily married life there is no room for hypocrisies and pretensions. The novelist at this point of the novel exposes the myth of a perfect happy wife and mother.

Jaya, though in her traditional role model upheld the idea to the maximum that "a husband is like a sheltering tree," she hardly thought of stepping out of his shadow. All her wants, desires, feelings had been nullified. She plays a perfect role of an ideal wife and looks after the comforts of her husband—his breakfast, lunch, tea and dinner. But, at the other end, Mohan keeps on demanding attention and care like any other husband, Mohan names Jaya as 'Suhasini' after their marriage. 'Suhasini' becomes the symbol of a painstaking and fastidious housewife, to only care and look after her children, maintain the home well and keep it in order. She feels that, she always has a supportive gesture towards her husband and family. Jaya is a gifted writer. But because Mohan does not like her writing and feels that through Jaya's writing, the people will know about their personal life, and hence restricts her writing career. Jaya very faithfully gives up her hobby and fits into the traditional role of an ideal wife. She even shuts her eyes to the corrupt practice of her husband. She compromises her creative, talented writing skills and writes silly and non-sensical things for a magazine in the 'Seeta' column. For him fiction is life, but for her life is a fiction, an illusion. This Seeta column, in course of time becomes a likable column for her female readers, Mohan and to her editors. Jaya sees in this Seeta column a patriarchal construct, "The means through which I had shut the doors, firmly, on all those women who invaded my being, screaming for my attention. Women...I could not write about, because they might...resemble Mohan's mother, or aunt, or my mother or aunt. Seeta was safer" (149). Jaya, deliberately gives up her creative aspect which is so close to her heart and negates her own self-accepting the role of a traditional housewife.

The third, last phase of feminism in the novel is Jaya's life —her articulation and assertion is hinted at the end of the novel to be the future possibility for Jaya. The whole exercise in the novel is for her eventual articulation, which will break her long silence. Strong hints are cited in the novel, that Jaya is going to break her passivity and even she asserts in these words, "I will have to erase the silence between us" (192).

The actual drama of breaking her silence is postponed to the future, this decision of hers, though not a drastic one is of a far-reaching significance. Surely the ice will break in the relationship of wife and husband. Her initiative in breaking 'The Long Silence,' is a welcome step towards restoring normalcy and happiness in the family. The early Indian tradition was that, men spoke a superior language and women were made to speak an inferior language, Jaya now realizes that, she was at fault by speaking 'Prakrit' when she could speak Sanskrit. She is continually oscillating between submission and assertion, the former is more dominant note in her character, is certainly not a prescriptive feminist character. Repeated accusations and allegations of Mohan force her to react sharply, "I was under attack. Questions rained on me. An adversary? Yes, that was what Mohan was, and an adversary more hostile than I had ever imagined" (116).

Mohan keeps on finding faults with Jaya—for not caring for his profession, his professional prospects, not looking after the wife of chief engineer, during his first posting at Lohanagar and the result was that, he lost the prospect of getting a better residential accommodation. He calls her completely selfish, "nothing mattered to you, only your needs, and you could see nothing else" (115).

He further criticizes her that she had married him because of her elder brother Dinkar (Dada). Even her fortnightly column 'Seeta,' Mohan tells her with his male ego, that it was he, who had always encouraged her to write the column 'Seeta'. It was he, who had first telephoned the editor of the "Woman's World". So that her silly scribbling pieces could be accepted. And that she is always silent during the current crisis of his professional life.

Jaya, in turn, bursts out and tells him that, she gave up creative writing because of the family, husband and two children. But when the quarrel continues longer than expected, she realizes that the bitter truth of frustration against each other had been cooking between them since long—"We've been silently weaving the threads of guilt, anger and resentment between us all these days" (115).

Jaya, right from day one of her marriage, till now concludes that her husband Mohan had never accepted her as Jaya (the victorious) but as he had renamed her as 'Suhasini'. He yearned for her to be soft spoken, obedient, always smiling, ready to serve, etc. But, when Jaya, in their fierce verbal battle, blurts out that—"Suhasini was dead; yes, that was it, she was the one Mohan was mourning.... No, the fact was that I'd finally done it—I'd killed her" (121).

It is only after she gets Mohan's telegram from Delhi informing her that everything is fine and their changed son Rahul's return, makes her think that she was silly in contemplating suicides earlier. She says—"I'm not afraid any more. The panic has gone. I'm Mohan's wife, I had thought, and cut off the bits of me that had refused to be Mohan's wife. Now I know that kind of a fragmentation is not possible" (191).

This feeling in her has a far-reaching significance; it will surely melt the ice in her relationship with her husband. Her step in breaking *That Long Silence* is towards restoring normalcy and happiness in the family. Between husband and wife, between members of the family no one's pride is at stake. All are one, belonging to a family. With promises of a happy life and of understanding between them, they decided that they will never make the same mistake again.

During her neurotic spell Jaya pours out her innermost secretive thoughts and thereby makes an unqualified confession of her 'sinful acts'. Till now she has never confided these sins even to her husband only because of her fear of jeopardising her marital security. She feels guilty about her clandestine fictional endeavours—"I had written even after that confrontation with him" (145). She is subconsciously gripped by the act of treachery against Mohan, for she had not allowed her third child to live. Though this was a long forgotten past, her enforced leisure aggravates her neurotic spell as it surfaces and torments her, "but now, as if it had been waiting for its cue all these years, a shadowy figure in the wings, guilt sprang out at me. I thought of the unborn child with dread and a piercing sorrow I invented her—yes, it would have been a girl—with all the qualities I missed in Rahul and Rati" (131).

Further we see that the novelist makes use of dreams as a literary device in a more subtle manner to describe symbolically and artistically the realities about the life of her heroines. Jaya's nightmares are the crucial turning points in her neurotic status revealing many conflicting tendencies within her. In one of her dreams, she sees Mohan and herself walking together where, suddenly she finds herself alone and has to pass through a house. She is helped into the house by a girl, which is empty, and no one is there to help her find Mohan. When she goes to another room, there are a number of girls but none of them help her. She feels ill and utterly helpless, and lies down like a dead body. The girls, in their low tones start talking about her predicament. Mohan appears and asks her to quicken towards a waiting taxi. But as she runs after Mohan, she realizes "that it is too late anyway, we will never be able to make it, and we will never be able get away. It is my entire fault" (86).

This dream expresses her entire marital experience, her present predicament and her unconscious wishes. No help comes to her, once she is inside her home, she alone has to make a house, and she has not understood Mohan fully. The catastrophe of the inquiry into the charges of corruption, the society which she had thought to be on her side, suddenly turns hostile. Her fall and degradation seems to be discussed by everyone like her younger brother Ravi, who talked to her about this issue. Followed by her neighbour Mukta's oblique reference to her unusual long stay at the Dadar flat, she repeatedly wishes to run away from her present predicament but tradition says that the wife should seek only her husband's help, so Mohan appears on the scene with a taxi. She is not sure of Mohan's ability of deliverance and therefore feels that it is very late, possibly the escape route is closed. She suffers a lot for she is unable to help Mohan in this hour of need and is only raving and grieving neurotically. If her first dream is that of wish fulfillment, her second dream much late is a sort of strong expression of utter frustration. Mohan has already deserted her and Jaya has to further shoulder this consequence of additional psychic conflict. Her maidservant Nayana's direct remarks about her pitiful plight further adds to Jaya's painful anguish. It is at this moment that Jaya recollects her 'crazy recurrent dream'—"I was looking for a toilet, I was desperate, I had to find one, I'd disgrace myself if I didn't find one at once. And yes, there it was—the immense relief, and then the overpowering shame as I realized I was in a public place surrounded by people staring at me steadily and silently" (161).

Jaya and Mohan had hoped to escape publicity by shifting into the Dadar flat. And Jaya in her dream unconsciously perceives her past experiences, which are stored at the back of her mind. Apprehension of disaster lurks deeply in her unconsciousness—"Why was it, I had often wondered that wars always, took place in other countries, tidal waves and earthquakes occurred in far-off, unknown places, that murder, adultery, and heroism had their places in other people's lives, never in ours?" (4). Hence, Jaya's tortured observation gives her an understanding that, a woman can never think of being angry, she can only be neurotic, hysterical and frustrated, so she slowly crawls to her safer comfortable, nice and smooth stories of Seeta. Mohan's desertion of Jaya makes her analyze her marital relationship, and knows that there was no romance or romantic time or sweet memories in their seventeen years of married life—"Love! No, I knew nothing of it. I knew only my need of Mohan and his need of me" (153).

In conclusion, it is observed that, the exigencies of life presented themselves in the form of traumatic events to Jaya, unveiling the predicament of human state. The novel compares the condition of those women who failed to voice and break their silence (like Kusum and Vimala) and finally Jaya thought of breaking her silence. The novel very authentically states that, the patriarchal set up is responsible for the women's condition in the Indian society. However, this is only partially true, for this responsibility also lies with the victims who refuse to raise a voice and achieve their goal. The novel, in a way is like a 'Multiple patchwork quilt of different elements'—facts that fictionalize and fiction that actualize. It is a patchwork, a collection of memories presented by myths and rituals, with a wide range of characters, situations, similar viewpoints, contrasting outlooks, all emotions, debating on life and art. The novel being a woman's version of her sense of world, tries to accommodate/place others viewpoints, and are oriented towards overall design of a woman's narration as a multiple patchwork quilt "is basically a woman's art". A women's narration is not claimed to be complete because she admits that man has his own understanding of the situation. Though her narrative is partial yet it is authentic. The novel moves from the nervous climax to the very reality of realities, it is an exploration of selfhood as a mere form of expression.

As it is often said and practiced that "Silence, tolerance, sufferance is golden" and though the novel is in the feminist framework, the novelist does not cross the limits of Indian, socio-cultural reality. In every sense, the novel is of immense relevance to us in the present day socio-cultural context. As Swain says, "The metaphor of silence under which the novel is organized helps to impose a quietude and discipline; the inner dynamics of a self-cut off from human communication. *That Long Silence* is not an intrusion into the world of silence but a silent communion with the oppressed self-straining for articulation, for a voice" (Swain, 2004).

Finally, Jaya understands that a holistic yet resilient approach towards life is necessary, "We don't change overnight. It's possible that we may not change even over long periods of time. But we can always hope. Without that, life would be impossible. And if there is anything I know now it is this: life has always to be made possible" (193). Her decision to cease to be a passive partner and overcome the turbulence in her relationship with Mohan leads her to an uninhibited self-identification. Thus, it has been rightly remarked that Deshpande, is concerned with a woman's quest for self-exploration into the female psyche and an understanding of the mysteries of life and the protagonist's place in it.

The novel clearly spells out the faith that a woman's desire to succeed like an individual does not negate her desire for love, marriage and domesticity. A balanced and purposeful life is not a utopian fancy for a woman if she liberates herself from the stereotyped conditioning of the society and is not dependent on the male presence to authenticate her thoughts and deeds at every step. *That Long Silence* aesthetically communicates the essence of the creed of feminism along with contemporary realities.

CROSSING LINES AND REAPPROPRIATING FEMALE SPACE IN ARUNDHATI ROY'S *THE GOD OF SMALL THINGS*

> A Feminine text cannot fail to be more than subversive. It is volcanic, as it is written it brings about an upheaval of the old property crust, carrier of masculine investments; there's no other way. There's no room for her if she's not a he. If she's a her-she, it's in order to smash everything, to shatter the framework of institutions, to blow up the law, to break up the "truth...".
>
> Hélène Cixous

In her essay, "Breaking Bounds in Arundhati Roy's *The God of Small Things*", Catherine Pesso-Miquel remarks, "Tomorrow", "les lendemains qui chantent", as the French say, will not come from liberalism but from those free souls who have rage and anger enough within them, and courage enough, to place themselves "on the dangerous edge of things", ...Progress will come from those courageous souls, helped and encouraged by the potent voice of literature. Arundhati Roy is one of them, both a brave, committed activist who is never afraid of breaking unjust bounds, and a delicate, gifted literary artist. [Catherine Pesso-Miquel, http://cle.ens-lyon.fr/anglais/breaking-bounds-in-arundhati-roy-s-the-god-of-small-things-121791.kjsp]

Arundhati Roy's novel, *The God of Small Things* evoked diverse opinions in academic and critical circles. If she was applauded by some as a female Rushdie, "establishing...the cultural striking back of the once-peripheral" (Boehmer 165) and raved over for her linguistic creativity and innovation with the English language, she was also lashed by some for her (negative) portrayal of the communist party in the novel (Mullaney 71). Apart from generating controversies as well as winning acclaim, Roy's novel has also been examined by scholars from diverse perspectives: feminist, postcolonial, post-structural, Marxist, etc. (see for example Boehmer 2005; Mullaney 2002; Pathak 2001).

In their introduction of *The Feminist Reader: Essays in Gender and the Politics of Literary Criticism* (1989) Catherine Belsey and Jane Moore suggest that while reading a text from a feminist point of view we should look at "how [it] represents women, what it says about gender relations, how it defines sexual difference" (Belsey and Moore 1). In "Arundhati Roy's *The God of Small Things: A Reader's Guide*," Julie Mullaney, propounds Roy's novel to be an manifestation of Gayatri Spivak's delineation of the 'Third World Woman' in her most controversial but best known essay, "Can the Subaltern Speak?" (11). Like Spivak before her, Roy too explores the diversity present among the native women. According to Mullaney, Roy examines the distinct, individual but closely interlaced lives of her female protagonists: Mammachi, Baby Kochamma, Ammu, Rahel, and the family cook, Kochu Maria. Rather than presenting them all as the oppressed "third world woman," Roy chooses to explore the wide range of options and choices, whether complicit, resistant, or both—to the dominant order which structures each of their individual life stories and their relation to the larger tessellations, familial, and cultural histories (11).

In this novel, Roy presents the lives of three generations of women who grapple with patriarchal oppression in several ways and contemplates on the "mutability and the continuity of certain forms of oppression" (Filipa da Silva 92). Mammachi and Baby Kochamma represent those women who have accepted their destiny; in fact, they have incorporated patriarchal values so completely that they even collaborate in the oppression of Ammu and her children. It is interesting to note how Mammachi and Baby Kochamma fit into the oppressive family system that openly victimizes Ammu. They become her active oppressors, seeking to corner her and drive her to her miserable death. One of the most glaring examples of it is the ambiguous stand adopted by these women with regard to Ammu's relation with Velutha. They express little sympathy for Ammu's lonely life, her tragic marital circumstances and her anxiety about her children. On the other hand, their casteist hostility finds double force in Ammu-Velutha liaison and breaks out into expressions of moral outrage while Chako's sexual indulgences with low caste women is overlooked as 'men's needs'. Ammu's affair with Velutha becomes an unpardonable offence against family's reputation and status. She was aware of his libertine relationships with the women in the factory, but had ceased to be hurt by them. When Baby Kochamma brought up the subject, Mammachi became tense and tight-lipped.

Ammu, as a spokeswoman of the second generation, is the character that pioneers rebellion while her daughter surfaces up as one who continues the fight for female liberation. Besides, Roy's novel doesn't centre solely on women who have been crushed by patriarchy but also presents a lower-class man (Velutha) as a victim of oppression. Roy's story is related from various points of view: through the eyes of those who were victimized by patriarchy—Estha and Rahel, and also through the eyes of the tragic lovers—Velutha and Ammu. Thus, Roy's novel succeeds in giving a voice to those people that would have been quietened by colonial and patriarchal discourse.

The aim of this essay is to critically examine Roy's novel from a postcolonial feminist perspective with a distinct emphasis on varying portrayals of women as victims of patriarchy. It also offers a commentary on native patriarchy and colonialism through Roy's characterization of both Pappachi and his son Chacko reminding us of Loomba's dictum regarding native men strengthening their position at home as an outcome of colonial dominance. In her book, Colonialism/Postcolonialism, Ania Loomba describes the pattern of the native men's behaviour at the time of colonialism: Colonialism intensified patriarchal oppression, often because native men, increasingly disenfranchised and excluded from the public sphere, became more tyrannical at home. They seized upon the home and the woman as emblems of their culture and nationality. The outside world could be Westernised but all was not lost if the domestic space retained its cultural purity (Loomba 141). What she describes in regard to colonialism can as well serve a depiction of the attitude towards women as described in Roy's novel. Ammu's husband, too, is convinced that once married he can treat her as he likes. Without any trace of discomfort he announces to her Mr. Hollick's offer, as though lending his wife to strangers was one of his rights. Being a woman is synonymous with being a man's property, a property that is at one point to be passed on to another person.

Marriage is in a way only a gift giving ritual that facilitates an appealing connection of two families.

The first section of this essay would focus on the three pivotal women characters and the second would focus on the aggressiveness with which patriarchal regimes treat women through the characters of Pappachi and Chacko.

The first and eldest of these three female characters is called Mammachi, the grandmother who is from a Syrian-Christian family. Her husband, Pappachi, the grandfather, hit Mammachi quite often with a brass-vase, leaving 'crescent shaped' scars on her skull. She has one daughter, Ammu, the black sheep of the family, and a son, Chacko a Rhodes-scholar, educated in Oxford. Mammachi starts a small business in making pickles and jams in her kitchen, a business her son Chacko soon takes control of and develops into a factory when he moves back home after his divorce. Mammachi idolizes her family as well as herself and has an almost compulsive obsession of grading every person she ever encounters, which usually ends up with them being located below her in the social stratum of her mind. Towards her husband, she reveals an ideal 'suffering wife' approach, submits herself to him, accepts her fate and directs her suppressed anger at other people, for example at Ammu, her defiant daughter. Mammachi is meek and passive towards people whom she believes to be superior to her, like her husband, and dictatorial to people she considers to be inferiors, like Ammu and her children. She tries to cover her oppressive impulses and be liberal and a good Christian towards Untouchables for instance, but this is merely a façade she has donned. Actually, she considers Untouchables to be at the lowest rung of the social ladder and is firmly grounded in the hierarchical caste system of her culture. This becomes apparent in her reaction towards Velutha when he crosses the boundary line and initiating a relationship with her own Touchable daughter. When Velutha's father approaches near her kitchen door, drunk and wretched, to acquaint her about the love affair, Mammachi begins to screech loudly, pushes him off the steps into the mud and spits at him, shouting "[d]runken Paravan liar" (243). When Velutha ultimately returns home the very evening, Mammachi loses her senses totally. She "spewed her blind venom, her crass, insufferable insults" (268) at him and used such an unbelievably offensive language that no one had ever heard her use earlier. Mammachi does not seem to mind the Untouchables educating themselves and working together with other Touchables of lower status than herself. A more severe limit encircles her own house and particularly her family; Velutha is not allowed to enter into the house, "except when she needed something mended or installed" (74), and certainly not permitted (unthinkable) to have a relationship with her daughter. When Mammachi comes face to face with the facts about his relationship with Ammu, the image of coupling dogs comes to her mind: "Like animals, [she] thought and nearly vomited. Like a dog with a bitch on heat" (244). The last thing Mammachi tells Velutha before he goes is: "If I find you on my property tomorrow I'll have you castrated like the pariah dog that you are! I'll have you killed!" (269).

Mammachi appears at first to be a very orthodox and submissive woman, but in fact she, in her own way, liberates herself from her husband although she never openly resists him. To start with, she starts her pickle business in the kitchen, though her husband Pappachi strongly disapproves of it. She is quite successful in the business which can only be regarded as a form of agency—that she gives a concrete shape to her idea inspite of her husband's and the local society's objections. Furthermore, after Chacko's interference against Pappachi's beatings, she is never beaten again and never again bothered by her husband. In fact, Pappachi and Mammachi exist like divorcées after that incident, only in the same house, but this type of relationship appears to suit Mammachi completely. Mammachi's liberation is definitely different from that of her daughter's—it is much more subtle and more indirect but all the same very important.

The next character, Baby Kochamma, is Mammachi's short but large sister-in-law and Ammu's aunt, much dreaded and detested by Ammu's children. In her youth, Baby Kochamma was quite defiant in the sense that she both challenged the tradition of arranged marriages by choosing a man herself, out of her own will, and then even converted to Catholicism against her father's will. However, later in life she apparently became more orthodox, and accepted her bad fate as a 'Manless woman' while denouncing others who shatter the rules like she once did. Evidently she pities herself and is jealous of other people, for instance Ammu, who as a "divorced daughter from an intercommunity love marriage" in Baby's opinion did not have the right to live in her parent's house. Baby Kochamma does not spare any chances to make Ammu and her twins understand this, but in her own, insinuating manner. She begrudges the twins every small moment of happiness and especially the "comfort they drew from each other" when they really ought to be generally unhappy and sad (45). This jealousy is probably a major motive behind Baby Kochamma's idea to return one of them (Estha) to their father after Ammu is kicked out of the house by Chacko. She is perhaps also envious of their relationship with Velutha, who has turned to be almost a father figure to them and reprimands Rahel for being "over-familiar" with Velutha (175). Another remarkable aspect of Baby Kochamma's character, is that she suffers from this "fear of being dispossessed", a political fear (shared with the elites and landowners worldwide) that keeps increasing every year. This fear, in her relation to Velutha, together with the age-old, more regional disdain towards Untouchables, generated strong feelings of antagonism that make her do almost anything to do away with him. On one occasion in the story, when the family's car is stuck in the midst of a Marxist demonstration, Baby Kochamma is embarrassed by a mob of men who make a joke out of her by compelling her to wave a red flag while yelling Marxist slogans. After this, she "focused all her fury at her public humiliation on Velutha" (78). "In her mind he grew to represent the march" and all that had been done to her, "all the men who had laughed at her" (78). It should be mentioned that Baby Kochamma's terror of the communists was not without cause. We are informed by the narrator that a new militant communist movement called the Naxalites spread rapidly across India and "struck terror in every bourgeois heart" (66) by arranging peasants into fighting cadres, throwing out landowners and capturing their land. They even set up "People's Courts" to bring "Class Enemies" to trial (66). In fact in Kerala, a landlord had been brutally hanged and killed recently. Even if the Ipe family is economically and socially on their decline, they bear the traits that easily would make them 'class-enemies' in the eyes of the Naxalites. Baby Kochamma is so terrorized by them that she, in her later years, locks all the doors and windows of the house, and even the fridge so that no one can steal her cream-buns.

As far as her relation with Velutha is concerned she is aware that Velutha is a person with the capability to transgress the boundaries of class and caste; an Untouchable with the looks and talents and brains to have 'a future' and without the common fears that regularly keep people in place in the hierarchy of society. She also considers Velutha a personal threat to her and to the entire family. Baby Kochamma has also more indirect ways of functioning. She has the dubious advantage of not having a man to submit to; her only love, the absent father Mullaney, does not impose any marital pressure on her other than the mental strain of being perpetually heartbroken. Therefore, Baby Kochamma is quite free to act according to her own mind, no matter how socially constructed this mind may be due to the customs and values of her community. She exercises power again and again to influence her surrounding according to her own beliefs. Protecting the honour of the family becomes a top priority to Baby Kochamma and she never ever hesitates to lie or manipulate others to achieve her goals. In fact, she has an incredible knack for explaining her actions by some higher aim, like when she consciously "misrepresented the relationship between Ammu and Velutha [by assuming rape], not for Ammu's sake, but to contain the scandal and salvage the family reputation in Inspector Thomas Mathew's eyes" (245). Another example of her clever manipulation is when Mammachi shows her anger towards Velutha. Baby Kochamma stands by her sister-in-law and says nothing but "used her hands to modulate Mammachi's fury, to stoke it anew. An encouraging pat on her back. A reassuring arm around the shoulders. Mammachi was completely unaware of the manipulation" (268).

Ammu is the rebellious daughter of the house, who succeeds in breaking free from her abusive father and subjugated, and overpowered mother by hastily accepting a marriage proposal from a Bengali Hindu man during a visit to a distant relative in Calcutta. Her prospective husband works as a tea estate assistant manager up in Assam and looks like a decent match to Ammu but unfortunately he turns out to be an alcoholic. However, after a couple of years in a terrible marriage she divorces him and moves back to Ayemenem with their two children, Estha and Rahel (two-egg twins), "to everything that she had fled from a few years ago. Except that now she had two young children. And no more dreams" (42). Ammu is most unwanted when she comes back to the house in Ayemenem and her father does not seem to trust her when she tells him about how her former husband wanted to sell her like a prostitute to save his own skin. Mammachi, who has tolerated years and years of beating and humiliation, is also quite dissatisfied with her rebellious, and now also divorced daughter. Baby Kochamma detests her more than anyone else because she feels that Ammu is "quarreling with a fate that she, Baby Kochamma herself, felt she had graciously accepted. The fate of the wretched Man-less woman" (44-45). In this scenario, Ammu falls in love with Velutha, who works as a carpenter in the pickle factory, and their love story forms the core of this novel.

Ammu is the most frankly rebellious character of the three; her experience from growing up with Pappachi's insulting and false ways striving to be regarded by society as a good and generous man while terrorizing his family at home made her develop a cautious attitude that made her suspect people's motives and actions. It also made her belligerent and combative; the narrator lets us know that she did "exactly nothing to avoid quarrels and confrontations, perhaps even enjoyed them" (173). These experiences motivate her to move against the tide and make choices over and over again that transgress all possible patterns and conventions enforced on her. Roy describes Ammu as being essentially 'herself' when she bursts out at someone whom she believes to act for example arrogant or dishonest. She "had not had the kind of education, nor read the sorts of books, nor met the sorts of people, that might have influenced her to think the way she did. She was just that sort of animal" (171). In these lines, Roy seems to convey that Ammu acts according to her 'essence', undeterred by society. However, we are also told about how Ammu's experiences during her adolescence influence and shape her, for instance about the "mulish, reckless streak that develops in Someone Small who has been bullied all their lives by Someone Big" (173). Ammu's parents show her the awful aspect of patriarchy and the terrible repurcussions of unquestioning female subjugation at its worst, urging her to choose to renounce and challenge it.

With her description of Ammu and Rahel, Roy creates two generations of strong defiant women. Jullie Mullaney argues that "Ammu and Rahel confound inherited models of femininity" (59). Thus, we see that, while the older generation, represented by Baby Kochamma and Mammachi, have come to terms with their destiny Ammu and Rahel refuse to submit; on the other hand, they stand up against patriarchal oppression. Filipa da Silva correctly remarks that Ammu and Rahel are motivating characters in that they make us ponder about the probability of emancipation and social reform (95).

Roy offers most of her assessment on colonial and patriarchal oppression through the character of Ammu. Ammu is best suited to voice that critique since she, as a woman, experiences what it is like to be pushed to the margins of society, or as Filipa da Silva phrases it; "she is then, because of her awareness of sexism, the better equipped to deconstruct colonial discourses" (80). A first example of her critical perspective can be found in her rejection of the family's wish to appear more 'British', which is considered synonymous with 'civilized'. Ammu realizes that this obsession to appear more civilized is a symptom of the Indian inferiority complex (Filipa da Silva 80). This feeling of inferiority had definitely been imposed upon them by the colonizers to such an extent that the colonized nation finally ended up adopting that same view. Ammu is very keen at exposing this incorrect construction of the Indian identity; for example, when the family is about to pick up Margaret Kochamma and Sophie Mol at the airport, Ammu resents the family's dramatic behaviour: "Must we behave like some damn godforsaken tribe that's just been discovered?" (Roy 180). Besides, she also condemns native patriarchy. Ammu looks upon her brother's proclaimed male superiority with great irony; therefore, when Mammachi tells her children the story of how a professor at Oxford said Chacko was "made of prime ministerial material" (*Ibid.* 56), Ammu rightly questions how a person who cannot even run a factory could run a whole country. She criticizes her brother's inability as the factory director and his abuse of the female labourers: "Just a case of a spoiled princeling playing Comrade! Comrade! An Oxford avatar of the old zamindar mentality—a landlord forcing his attentions on women who depended on him for their livelihood" (*Ibid.* 65). She considers her brother to be a typical male chauvinist who does not acknowledge her contributions to the family business. Filipa da Silva rightly remarks that Ammu's "remarks create a critical space to think outside of colonial discourse" (80).

Ammu offers us an alternative perspective that exposes the subjugated position women hold in a patriarchal society. In doing so, she assists in reconstructing the silenced woman's voice. Even in her behaviour, as we have seen before, Ammu defies female oppression. Ammu's first act of rebellion consists in marrying a Bengali man out of love. Baba is deemed unsuitable for a girl like Ammu because he does not belong to the same community and because he was not selected by her parents. In addition, she defies tradition by daring to divorce her abusive husband and by claiming a place for herself and her children in her parents' house. She therefore brings defamation to her entire family. Her major rebellious deed, which will ultimately cause her to surrender everything, consists in falling in love with the untouchable Velutha. By opting to love another man after her first marriage, Ammu is said to "refuse a sex-less, body-less identity only because she was a divorced mother" (Filipa da Silva 96). Indeed, unlike her aunt Baby Kochamma, who "graciously accepted" (Roy 45) her fate, Ammu does not want to become a "wretched Man-less woman" (*Ibid.* 45). After all, she was only twenty-seven years old at the time of her love affair with Velutha.

Like her mother before her, Rahel is an emblem of female rebellion. Ever since she was a child, she is said to have a rebellious nature. For example, she is blacklisted for the first time after having decorated the Housemistress's doorknob with cow dung. We also come to know that she is expelled from school for the third time after "setting fire to her Housemistress's false hair bun" (Roy 17). The teachers also believe that Rahel is a strange child that does not seem to "know how to be a girl" (*Ibid.* 17). At home, too, she and her brother quite often violate the rules. It is said, for example, that the twins are reprimanded when they utter their mother tongue, Malayalam and are forced to use their English pronunciation—"Prer NUN sea ayshun" (*Ibid.* 36) by Baby Kochamma. However, they try out ways to defy through inventive language games like reading backwards. Cynthia Vanden Driesen reads the twins language games as "a powerful subversion of the established order: they read the word as they read the world in oppositional mode to that ordained by the powers that be" (qtd. in Mullaney 65). In discussing Rahel's rebellion, it is important to see that she is paired off with her twin brother Estha; Arundhati Roy makes them mystify gender roles. When the family is watching The Sound of Music, for instance, Estha is compared to Julie Andrews singing "in a nun's voice, as clear as clean water" (Roy 101) while Rahel identifies most with the male protagonist Captain von Trapp. Another example showing Estha dressing up as a Hindu woman together with his sister and cousin as part of a game. He is believed to be "the draping expert" (*Ibid.* 189). A much more painful example of feminization, as Julie Mullaney argues, is the fact that Estha becomes the victim of sexual abuse (59). As a result, Estha withdraws into silence, becoming "a quiet bubble floating on a sea of noise" (Roy 11). By turning into the 'silent other', I think that he assumes the role similar to many victimized women. At his father's home Estha also refuses to utilize his male privileges; instead, he behaves like a female servant carrying out household chores "much to the embarrassment of his father and stepmother" (*Ibid.* 11). His sister, on the other hand, takes on a more powerful position than is expected from a girl by following in her mother's footsteps. As an adult, she also challenges the traditional female role enforced by patriarchy by choosing a husband for herself from outside the community and by divorcing him later on. During the period of her childhood and adolescence, Rahel is ignored by Mammachi and Chacko:

"They provided the care (...) but withdrew the concern" (Roy 15). There is no dowry arranged for her, like there was none for her mother. However, "neglect seemed to have resulted in an accidental release of the spirit" (*Ibid.* 17). Thus, Rahel can partly be visualised as a reflection of the author. Roy had remarked, "I thank God that I had none of the conditioning that a normal, middle class Indian girl would have. I had no father, no presence of this man telling us that he would look after us and beat us occasionally in exchange" (Roy Interview). Roy's words are apt for Rahel too: without a father—or anyone else for that matter—around to fix a marriage for her, Rahel is independent to take her own decision: "she remained free to make her own enquiries (...) into life and how it ought to be lived" (Roy 17). When she arrives in Ayemenem, Rahel has the same age as Ammu when she died and she has by then also divorced her husband. Her arrival implies a new beginning; motivated by her mother's example, Rahel will continue the fight for female emancipation where her mother discontinued.

Thus, we see that Roy presents varying female characters in her novel *The God of Small Things*, who are all projected as victims of patriarchal oppression but also display an appreciable measure of agency. She has dared to give utterance to some of those who are rarely visible in the official history writing of India. From a postcolonial feminist perspective Roy has contributed to make the representation of the Third World subaltern woman more diverse, through giving us various portraits of women that, despite their oppressed and marginalized status, are not depicted without agency or responsibility. The woman who most clearly rejects the intricate system of oppression in the story, Ammu, is punished severely by her mother and aunt. But as one of the main characters in Roy's novel, Ammu exemplifies people who actually venture to do 'the unthinkable', to trespass the very line that endorses the system of difference that casteism essentially upholds. She epitomises all those who have suffered due to violations against the 'Love Laws' and gender-specific expectations forced upon them, at times even by sacrificing their own lives. Championing the portrayal of thousands of cross-caste relationships in the real India, the saga of Ammu and Velutha, continues to echo in every corner of the world.

I will now examine the aggressiveness with which colonial and patriarchal setups treat women through an analysis of the characters of Pappachi and Chacko. Pappachi violently hits his wife and daughter while preserving the image of the perfect man, an abider of English civilization, in the public arena: "He worked hard on his public profile as a sophisticated, generous, moral man. But alone with his wife and children he turned into a monstrous, suspicious bully, with a streak of vicious cunning. They were beaten, humiliated and then made to suffer the envy of friends and relations for having such a wonderful husband and father" (Roy 180).

Chacko is fortunate enough to be send away to school, while little Ammu has to tolerate her overbearing father daily. Mammachi got accustomed to being beaten by her husband; she "suffered those beatings with mute resignation" (Roy 180); for example, at the funeral of Pappachi Ammu clarifies to the children that Mammachi is crying "more because she was used to him than because she loved him. She (...) was used to being beaten from time to time" (*Ibid.* 50). Here, Roy is condemning the manner in which the postcolonial, patriarchal society makes its women accept patriarchal values up to a level where brutal exploitation is taken for granted. Now, like his father before him, Chacko is on the margins of both English civilization and his native culture. He is "caught (...) between the newly independent India represented by Mammachi's 'Paradise Pickles & Preserves' and the model of England and Englishness inherited via Pappachi and his own Oxford education" (Mullaney 34). He completely exemplifies the postcolonial citizens who are seized between two very different cultures and how they never actually adapt into either one of these cultures. Chacko elaborates the colonial repurcussion on the family to the twins by clarifying that they "were a family of Anglophiles. Pointed in the wrong direction, trapped outside their own history, and unable to retrace their steps because their footprints had been swept away" (Roy 52). This portrait of footprints being swept away also resurfaces in the predicament of Velutha's survival as a paravan: "He left no footprints in sand, no ripples in water, no image in mirrors" (Roy 265). Through the footprints imagery, Roy is perhaps condemning Chacko for failing to acknowledge that he, as a representative of the postcolonial order, is equally responsible and a party to the oppression of the 'other'—the 'other' comprising of Velutha as well as his own mother, his sister and her children. At first, Chacko comes up as his mother and sister's defender and in doing so wins Mammachi's enduring admiration: "Mammachi packed her wifely luggage and committed it to Chacko's care" (Roy 168). However, just like his father Pappachi, Chacko very soon becomes the dictatorial head of the house. First of all, he takes over control of his mother's small pickles business, thus taking away "what was hers alone" (Mullaney 37). He develops it into a huge factory called "Paradise Pickles & Preserves". His inadequacy soon brings his mother's booming business in economic crisis, which he tries to solve by mortgaging the family's rice fields. If Mammachi's production of pickles epitomizes the idea of postcolonial independence, then the takeover by Chacko—who exemplifies native patriarchy—projects the failure of the postcolonial state to carry through those ideals (Mullaney 40). Secondly, Chacko vindicates the demise of his daughter by exploiting the most defenceless and sensitive people in the family: his sister Ammu, who has no legal standing, and her two innocent children. He accuses them for what happened and together with Baby Kochamma, makes arrangement for them to be sent away: Ammu is prohibited from the house, compelled to live in poverty, which will finally cause her to die; Estha is sent away to live with his father, the final appalling experience which literally quietens him for ever; and Rahel is sent from one boarding school to another because she is always being expelled for her defiant behaviour. Chacko himself ultimately shifts to Canada, where he ironically initiates an antique business, which symbolically indicates towards the fact that he is stuck in the past. In short, by making Pappachi a representative of the old colonial regime and representing Chacko as someone of the new postcolonial generation, perhaps Roy wants to show how nothing has changed regarding the treatment of women; the postcolonial state just lingered the oppression by the colonial regime rather than bring any change.

The first aspect through which Roy derides the patriarchal oppression of women can be seen in the educational opportunities offered or denied to the women in the novel. The first woman who is denied an education is Mammachi. As a married woman, she is not permitted to any sort of education as becomes apparent, for example, when Pappachi prohibits her to prolong her violin lessons: "The lessons were abruptly discontinued when Mammachi's teacher (...) made the mistake of telling Pappachi that his wife was exceptionally talented and, in his opinion, potentially concert class" (Roy 50). As a woman of the second generation, Ammu is no improvement on her mother: she is denied any college education as her father thinks it to be "an unnecessary expense for a girl" (*Ibid.* 38). Baby Kochamma is only permitted to pursue ornamental gardening in the United States because she "was unlikely to find a husband" (*Ibid.* 26) after exhibiting her love for father Mulligan and her consequent conversion to Catholicism. Her father decides that "since she couldn't have a husband there was no harm in her having an education" (*Ibid.* 26). Thus, we see that, education is considered to be a harmful tool for a prospective bride. In bringing out this sensitive issue, Roy is attempting to expose how the denial of education serves to keep women into submission; they remain dependent upon their husband. Rahel, on the other hand, seems to be able to enjoy more freedom than the women before her. Since there is no dominant figure around in her life who makes decisions for her, she is able to obtain a place at a College of Architecture in Delhi. Even though she doesn't complete her degree, the opportunity to study makes her to more independent: she is free to do what she wants, far away from the authoritative regime of Mammachi and Chacko.

In her critique of Indian patriarchies, Roy also focuses on the status of divorced women in Indian society. The traditional system does not provide for this "anomaly" as Filipa da Silva (94) calls it; these women do not have room to exist: "wives 'endure', they don't 'divorce'" (*Ibid.* 94). Since Ammu's father does not have the necessary money to furnish a dowry, she cannot find a husband and is doomed to become an old spinster caught in her parents' house. In her desolation, she manages to convince her father to let her spend a summer with an aunt in Calcutta where she meets her future husband. Marriage is her option of evading her father's abuse; however, as we learn later on, her new husband turns out to be an alcoholic who beats her as well.

Ammu opposes tradition by divorcing her alcoholic, abusive husband when she learns that he wants to offer her to his boss in lieu of keeping his job. She then decides to move back to her parents' home. Not only is she unwanted there because she is a divorced woman, but her father also refuses to trust her story: "He didn't believe that an Englishman, any Englishman, would covet another man's wife" (Roy 42). Pappachi's faith in the moral superiority of the former colonizers is so immense that he does not seem read his daughter's pain. Ammu's existence in the Ayemenem house is seen as something disgraceful for varied reasons: "(...) a married daughter had no position in her parent's home. As for a divorced daughter—according to Baby Kochamma, she had no position anywhere at all. And as for a divorced daughter from a love marriage, well, words could not describe Baby Kochamma's outrage. As for a divorced daughter from a [sic] intercommunity love marriage—Baby Kochamma chose to remain quiveringly silent on the subject" (*Ibid.* 45-46).

Filipa da Silva explains that in India, "daughters are not their parents' responsibility beyond childhood" (91) because being married means becoming part of the husband's family for the rest of your life. It is emphatically stated in the novel that Ammu has "no Locusts Stand I" (Roy 57), meaning that she has no legal position as a divorced woman nor as a daughter. Roy expresses her assessment on this marginal position of women in society by examining the disparity in treatment between the pampered son Chacko and the detested daughter Ammu. Chacko is allowed to study at Oxford College whereas Ammu does not receive any educational opportunity. Besides, Ammu has no lawful claim to the family business because she is a girl. She contributes as much as her brother but is not considered his equal, as Chacko clearly explains to Ammu: "What's yours is mine and what's mine is also mine" (Roy 57). Ultimately, Chacko's umpteen love affairs are easily excused in the name of "Men's Needs" (*Ibid.* 168) whereas the family decides to interfere when Ammu falls in love with the untouchable Velutha. A divorced woman who falls in love with a paravan is considered to be a great disgrace for the family so their relationship should be terminated straight away. Ammu's secluded position within the family is visible in the scene of Sophie Mol's funeral in which she along with her children are made to stand at a distance from the rest of the family (Filipa da Silva 95).

Ammu's disgraceful behaviour also influences the lives of her twins Estha and Rahel. Mullaney remarks that "as children of mixed ancestry and divorced parents Rahel and Estha fall between traditions (Hindu and Syrian Christians) and are afforded no real recognition of what the novel calls 'Locusts Stand I' (legal standing)" (31). Moreover, we learn that Ammu refused to give her children a surname, which means that they are unclaimed (*Ibid.* 31): For the Time Being they had no surname because Ammu was considering reverting to her maiden name, though she said that choosing between her husband's name and her father's name didn't give a woman much of a choice (Roy 36-37).

The twins' existence in the Ayemenem house "is a continuous source of embarrassment for the family" (Filipa da Silva 94). Estha and Rahel's existence invariably reminds the other family members of how Ammu ventured to divorce her husband and assert a place for her and her children in her parents' house. As Filipa da Silva puts it: they are "the living testimony of Ammu's failure to live up to expected patterns of decency and convenience" (94). The other adults in the house believe that the children are not their responsibility since the twins are staying in the 'wrong' family. One of the remarks of Kochu Maria, the house servant, shows how the children are not welcomed there: "'Tell your mother to take you to your father's house,' (...). 'There you can break as many beds as you like. These aren't your beds. This isn't your house'" (Roy 83). After the unfortunate events the family decides to separate Estha and Rahel because "together they were trouble" (Roy 302). Estha is therefore sent away to stay with his father. The continual pressure of the family about how the children need a father in their lives ultimately even shakes Ammu's original decision to bring up the twins without a man: "Maybe they're right (...). Maybe a boy does need a Baba" (Roy 302).

Roy tries to challenge patriarchal oppression by portraying the transgression of the 'Love Laws' made by Ammu and Velutha on the one hand, and the second generation lovers Estha and Rahel on the other hand. Filipa da Silva sees the erotic transgression in the novel as a political act (83). Indeed, by falling in love with an untouchable, Ammu is disobeying the social laws, the "Love Laws" that "lay down who should be loved. And how. And how much" (Roy 177). As an untouchable, Velutha is not supposed to be loved, especially not by a woman from a higher caste like Ammu. Unfortunately, the affair has terrible consequences for both lovers. When Mammachi first hears about the love affair she is utterly sickened by the thought of it: Her tolerance of 'Men's Needs' as far as her son was concerned, became the fuel for her unmanageable fury at her daughter. She had defiled generations of breeding (...) and brought the family to its knees. For generations to come, for ever now, people would point at them at weddings and funerals. At baptisms and birthday parties. They'd nudge and whisper. It was all finished now (Roy 258).

In their rage, Mammachi and Baby Kochamma imprison Ammu in her room and send the police after Velutha. When Ammu hears about their false accusations, she goes to the police herself to "try and set the record straight" (Roy 259). However, as a woman without a legal standing, she is quickly dismissed by the police. After her children are taken away from her, she is banned from the house by Chacko. Ammu ends up living in poverty and eventually dies all alone. Filipa da Silva argues that "Ammu is (...) to a certain extent, a 'failed' model of transgression because she follows the traditional narrative scheme of shame, marginalisation and death" (96). The love affair indeed turns out to be disastrous for both lovers as they both die. However, I refuse to see their deaths as a failure to escape the established order. Their transgression can be read as a powerful attempt to break with the established order and to give a voice to the most marginalized people in Indian society:

women and paravans. Moreover, their act of rebellion has not been in vain because the next generation—represented by Ammu's children Estha and Rahel—is ready to take over and continue the struggle. Estha and Rahel are symbolically thirty-one years old, the same age as their mother when she died. As Filipa da Silva points out, this "circularity of time (...) suggests that the twins are starting off where former rebels left" (87).

In conclusion, I think that *The God of Small Things* is an extraordinary novel in which Roy staunchly denounces the unfair treatment of women by the established patriarchal order through an analysis of the peripheral position of three generations of women. Not only does she acquaint the reader with the ways in which women are exploited by men, an exploitation which often goes together with violent abuse, but she also presents the examples of female resistance against that patriarchal oppression.

In Roy's novel, all the main, transgressive characters—Ammu, Velutha, Estha and Rahel—resist stereotypical gender roles and reach out to each other across the boundaries of gender and caste. They are critical of the norms of the patriarchal society and its codes of conduct, and attempt to create an existence outside that tyrannical patriarchal structure. In this attempt, they become inspirational figures who indicate various directions for social change.

Works Cited

Allen and Unwin, 1987. Print.

Anzaldua, G. (1990). La consciencia de la mestiza [The conscience of the Mestiza]: Towards a new consciousness. In G. Anzaldua (Ed.), *Making Face, Making Soul: Creative and Critical Perspectives of Feminists of Color* (377-89). San Francisco: Aunt Lute Books.

Belsey, Catherine and Moore, Jane. *The Feminist Reader: Essays in Gender and the Politics of Literary Criticism*. Malden: Macmillan, 1989. Print.

Bhasin, Kamala, and Nighat Khan Said. "Some Questions on Feminism and Its Relevance in South Asia," *Kali for Women*, New Delhi, 1986.

Boehmer, Elleke. *Stories of Women. Gender and Narrative in the Postcolonial Nation*. Manchester: Manchester University Press, 2005. Print.

Bowen, S. and Wyatt, N. (Eds.) (1993). *Transforming Visions: Feminist Critiques in Communication Studies*. Cresskill, NJ: Hampton Press.

Butler, J. (1990). *Gender Trouble*. New York: Routledge.

Caine, Barbara et al., eds. (1998). *Australian Feminism: A Companion*. Melbourne: Oxford University Press.

Chaudhuri, Maitrayee. ed. "Feminism in India: Issues in Contemporary Indian Feminism," *Kali for Women*, New Delhi, 2004.

Connell, R.W. (1995). *Masculinities*. Berkeley: University of California Press.

——. *Gender and Power: Society, the Person and Sexual Politics*. Australia.

Delmar, Rosalind (1986). "What Is Feminism?" in Juliet Mitchell and Ann Oakley, eds. *What Is Feminism*? New York: Pantheon Books.

Deshpande, Shashi. Quoted in the online edition of *The Hindu*, Aug. 28, 2003: Breaking *That Long Silence*.

——. "I'm not a feminist: Shashi Deshpande". *The Times of India*, News Service, 22 Jul. 2001.

——. *That Long Silence*. New Delhi: Penguin Books, 1988. All textual citations in the article kept in parentheses are from this edition of the novel.

Dicker, R. and Piepmeier, A. (2003). *Catching a Wave: Reclaiming Feminism for the 21st Century*. Boston: Northeastern University Press.

Douglas, Susan. *Where the girls are*. Three Rivers Press, 1995: 273.

Echols, Alice. *Daring to be Bad: Radical Feminism in America*, 1967-1975. U of Minnesota, 1989.

Faludi, Susan, *Backlash: The Undeclared War Against Women*. Broadway, 2006: 15.

Filipa da Silva de Melo Vilela Passos, Joana. "*Arundhati Roy*". *Micro-universes and Situated Critical Theory: Postcolonial and Feminist Dialogues in a Comparative Study of Indo-English and Lusophone Women Writers*. Diss. University of Utrecht, 2003. 26 Apr. 2010. <http://igitur-archive.library.uu.nl/dissertations/2003-0310-101002/pt2c2.pdf>

Freud, Sigmund, "Femininity" in *New Introductory Lectures on Psychoanalysis*, tr. James Strachey (New York, Norton, 1965): 112.

Friedan, B. (1974). *The Feminine Mystique*. New York: Dell.

Gaard, G. and Gruen, L. (1993). Ecofeminism: Toward global justice and planetary health. Feminism and ecology issue. *Society and Nature: The International Journal of Political Ecology*, 2, 1-35.

Glover, David and Cora Kaplan, *Genders*, [2nd edition], (London & New York: Routledge, 2009): 26.

Griffin, G.B. (1992). *Calling: Essays on teaching in the mother tongue*. Pasadena, CA: Trilogy Books.

Griffin, Gabrielle, Hennessy, Rosemary, Jackson, Stevi and Roseneil, Sasha (2000). 'Editorial' *Feminist Theory* 1(1), April: 5-9.

Guy-Sheftall, B. (2006). "African Feminisms: The Struggle Continues". In C. Berkin, J.L. Pinch, and C.S. Appel (Eds.), *Exploring Women's Studies: Looking Forward, Looking Back* (25-37). Upper Saddle River, NJ: Pearson Prentice-Hall.

Halbert, Debra. *Shulamith Firestone*. Information, Communication & Society 2004 March 7(1): 115-35.

Haraway, D.J. (1991). *Simians, Cyborgs, and Women: The Reinvention of Nature*. New York: Routledge.

Hariharan, Githa. Interview with Arnab Chakladar. "A Conversation with Githa Hariharan." September 2005.

Hooks Bell, *Ain't I a Woman: Black Women and Feminism*, South End Press, 1999, 195.

Humm, Maggie (1989). *The Dictionary of Feminist Theory*. Hemel Hempstead, Hertfordshire: Harvester Wheatsheaf.

Jardine, Alice (1985). *Gynesis: Configurations of Woman and Modernity*, Ithaca and London: Cornell University Press.

Kapur, Manju. Interview with Kiran Nagarkar. Love Marriages: "Too Much Adjustment." 7 June 2006. http://www.rediff.com/news/2006/jun/07spec1.htm

King, Adele: "Effective Portrait". *Debonair*, June 1988: 97.

Kolawole, M. (1997). *Womanism and African Consciousness*. Trenton, NJ: African World Press.

Leavant, B. and E. Santra (1999). *Same Sex Domestic Violence: Strategies for Change*. New Delhi: Sage, 1999.

Leitch, Vincent B. *American Literary Criticism from the Thirties to the Eighties*. Columbia: UP, 1988: 308.

Loomba, Ania. *Colonialism/Postcolonialism: The New Critical Idiom*. 2nd ed. Oxon: Routledge, 2005.

Mill, John Stuart. "On the Subjection of Women." *The Norton Anthology of English Literature*. M.H. Abrams et al. Vol. 2. Norton, 1974: 989-98.

Millard, Elaine. "French Feminism." *Feminist Readings/Feminists Reading*. Sara Mills et al. Harvester P., 1989, 155.

Millett, Kate. *Sexual Politics*. N.Y.: Doubleday, 1970.

Mullaney, Julie. *The God of Small Things: A Reader's Guide*. New York: Continuum, 2007.

Offen, Karen (1988). "Defining Feminism: A Comparative Historical Approach", *Signs* 14(1), Autumn: 119-57.

Oyewumi, O. (Ed.) (2003). *African Women and Feminism: Reflecting on the Politics of Sisterhood*. Trenton, NJ: African World Press.

Pleck, K.H. (1995). "The gender role strain paradigm: An update." In R.E. Leyant and W.S. Pollack, eds., *A New Psychology of Men*. New York: Basic Books.

Ramamoorthi, P. "My Life is My Own: A Study of Shashi Deshpande's Women." *Feminism and Recent Fiction in English*. ed. Sushila Singh. New Delhi: Prestige Books, 1991: 115.

Redefining the F-word, Special Report—Sunday TOI—Home, 3 Jan. 2010, timesofindia.indiatimes.com.

Robins, Elizabeth. A Speech in WWSL, 1907. Quoted in *That Long Silence* by Shashi Deshpande. New Delhi: Penguin Books, 1989. Epigraph.

Roy, Arundhati. Interview with David Barsamian. The Progressive Apr. 2001. 10 May 2010 <http://www.progressive.org/intv0401.html>

——. *The God of Small Things*. 1997. London: Harper Perennial, 2004.

Ruthven, K.K. *Feminist Literary Studies*. Cambridge University Press, 1984: 16.

Sinha, Sunita. *Post-Colonial Women Writers: New Perspectives*. New Delhi: Atlantic, 2008: 221-22.

Smith, Barbara, in *This Bridge called my back: Writings by Radical Women of Colour*, ed. Cherrie Moraga and Gloria Anzaldua, Watertown, MA: Persephone Press, 1981: 63.

Spencer, Sharon. "Feminist Criticism and Literature." *American Writing Today*. ed. Richard Kostelanetz. Forum Series 2. Washington D.C: 1982: 157.

Spivak, Gayatri Chakravorty. *Can the Subaltern Speak?* (1988) Rev. ed. reprinted in Can the Subaltern Speak? Reflections on the History of an Idea. 21-78. Ed. Rosalind C. Morris. New York: Columbia University Press, 2010: 21-78. Print.

Swain, S.P. "Articulation of the Feminine Voice: Jaya in Shashi Deshpande's *That Long Silence*." *Shashi Deshpande: A Critical Spectrum*. ed. T.M.J. Indra Mohan. Delhi: Atlantic, 2004: 96.

Tong, Rosemary (1989). *Feminist Thought: A Comprehensive Introduction* London: Unwin Hyman.

Tong, R.P. (1998). *Feminist Thought* (2nd ed.). Boulder CO: Westview.

Walker, R. (1992, January/February). Becoming the third wave. *Ms. Magazine*, 39-41.

Walters, Margaret. *Feminism: A Very Short Introduction*. Oxford University, 2005.

Warren, K.J. (1993). The power and the promise of ecological feminism. In M.E. Zimmerman, J.B. Callicott, G. Sessions, K.J. Warren, and J. Clark (Eds.), *Environmental philosophy: From animal rights to radical ecology* (320-41). Englewood Cliffs, NJ: Prentice-Hall.

Weedon, Chris. "Quotation from Narayan." *On Dislocating, Cultures: Identities, Traditions and Third World Feminism*. New York: Routledge, 1997: 13.

Wollstonecraft, M. (1975). *A Vindication of the Rights of Women*. In C.H. Poston (Ed.), New York: Norton. (Original work published 1792).

Woolf, Virginia. *A Room of One's Own*. Harvester, 1981: 52.

Chapter 3
Narrating Queerness

> "Queer is by definition whatever is at odds with the normal, the legitimate, the dominant."
>
> David Halperin (1995)

Gender studies and queer theory explore issues of sexuality, power, and marginalized populations (woman as other) in literature and culture. In recent years, the term 'queer' has come to be used as an umbrella term for a coalition of culturally marginal sexual self-identifications and at other times to depict a burgeoning arena which has blossomed forth out of the traditional lesbian and gay studies. As 'queer' is not associated with any specific identity category, it has the flexibility to be annexed profitably to any number of discussions. The meteoric development and incorporation of lesbian and gay studies in universities in the 1990s is matched by an increasing deployment of the term 'queer'. Queer includes those actions which magnify incoherencies in the avowedly stable relations between chromosomal sex, gender and sexual desire—the mismatches between sex, gender and desire. Institutionally, queer has been associated most prominently with lesbian and gay subjects, but its logical configuration also includes such topics as cross-dressing, hermaphroditism, gender ambiguity and gender-corrective surgery. For Halperin, queer is a way of pointing ahead without knowing for certain what to point at. "Queer"...does not designate a class of already objectified pathologies or perversions, writes Halperin; "rather, it describes a horizon of possibility whose precise extent and heterogenous scope cannot in principle be delimited in advance" (Halperin 1995). Queer is always an identity under construction, a site of permanent becoming. As Lee Eldeman remarks, "utopic in its negativity, queer theory curves endlessly toward a realization that its realization remains impossible" (Eldeman 1995). Thus, we see that, Queer Studies is a relatively new field, emerging in the 1990s, which draws upon the ideas and *modus operandi* from anthropology, history, geography, psychology, sociology, literature, philosophy, political theory, biology, art, and art history, religious studies, science and technology studies, performance studies, and visual studies. It shares intellectual affinities with the interdisciplinary fields of women's studies, gender studies, ethnic studies, critical legal studies, and cultural studies. Various perceptions from area studies, religious studies, science and technology studies, and visual studies also enrich this field of study.

On July 2, 2009, the Delhi High Court gave a judgment in favour of the Naz Foundation, an organization that works for same-sex equality, affirming that the application of Section 377 of the Indian Penal Code that condemned consensual sex among adults was illegal. The decriminalization of homosexuality enacted by the landmark decision was repealed in part—it retained non-consensual sex as criminal—the colonial penalization of same-sex practices brought in by T.B. Macaulay in 1860 that banned "carnal intercourse against the order of nature with any man, woman or animal" (qtd. in Narrain and Elridge 9). Heralded as a "great victory over an archaic and bizarre law," the victorious consummation of a decade long political mobilization created a distinct temporal divide between pre- and post-2009 queer activism in India (Gay Ruling). To Kajal Bhardwaj, this verdict was a model of "the ultimate vision of India—a society based on inclusiveness" (99). It marks a step ahead further in the process of decolonization from inherited homophobic laws in postcolonial India.

In today's context, it is significant to begin with Bhupen Khakar's painting, *Two Men in Benaras* as the most apt "visual" manifesto of a new generation of Indian artists who are increasingly using their tools to disclose fresh intimacies of human relations and dare new challenges to social constraints. Khakar is the only Indian a painter who is openly homosexual though he is not a gay activist. His works reflect his own personal view and are not meant to make a social or cultural statement. The painting shows two men in naked embrace as the Ganges flows around their lust in the landscape of sadhus, thus conjoining genitals and religious setting.

The religious sense of sexuality is nothing new in the Indian fiction, as it remains a perennial preoccupation of Hindu culture, expressed both in erotic flourishes of Indian art and in ancient rituals of its popular religion. An opportune moment to start talking about Indian sexuality would be Vatsayayana's celebrated text *Kamasutra*. In reference to non-normative sexual practices, the text responds, "in all things connected with love, everybody should act according to the custom of the country, and his own inclination" (Burton 1994: 127). Classic texts such as the Kamasutra not only described but even prescribed 'queer' sexual practices such as 'auparishtaka' or mouth congress (*Ibid.* 70). What is important to consider about this text is that sexual practices discussed do not necessarily head towards procreation but rather pleasure. Thus non-procreative sexual practice, a form of non-normative or queer deviation from prescribed sexual practice is represented within ancient India. One of the liminalities of sexuality studies of this period is the absence of precolonial laws around queer sexuality. The Hindu religion is complex because of the several types of religious life that existed in ancient India. The *Manusmriti* (Laws of Manu), one of the earliest treatise on Hindu law prohibits men from practicing 'ayoni' (non-vaginal) sex. However, there has been no evidence found so far of anyone being executed or punished in ancient India for same sex relations (Vanita and Kidwai 2000).

It is also relevant to mention here, Hoshang Merchant—poet, academic and editor of a daring anthology of gay writings who says, Hindu culture treats homosexuality "with secrecy but not with malice" (Merchant 1999: xii). Merchant further elaborates, "Homosexuality as it is known in the West, does not exist in India" (Merchant 1999: xii). In India, most homosexuals resort to a conventional married life, easily adjusting themselves to a double life and inventing a further version of 'arranged marriage' based on painful compromises so as to conform to societal pressures. According to Merchant, strong male bonding has always been prevalent in India. We find possibility of homosexuality among Brahmin boys in South India, as for them girls mensuration is a taboo and compels them to be attracted to other men. Secondly, the *guru shishya parampara* has platonic relationships but what is also evident is a gender conundrum in some tales of Mahabharata like, for example, the Kannada tale, *The Prince Who Married His Own Left Half*, the beginning of which is as under:

> The king had a son. When the prince came of age, the king wished to get him married, but the young man didn't want to get married. He listened to no one's advice, not even to the elders'. The father became rather desperate and threatened to hang himself if the prince didn't get married. The son then said, "All right. Split my body in two and bury my left half in flowers. A woman will be born out of it. I'll marry her. I won't marry anyone else." (Ramanujan 1997: 142)

The tale tells of an unfaithful wife, or rather a man's own feminine self, burnt to passion for another man who in turn has to disguise himself in the shape of a snake to her/him in secrecy, change into a man again and finally consume their love but the snake lover is dead and therefore the inconsolable feminine half of the prince has to kill his 'male other' to free herself. As the prince dies, his wife who was his own left half took another lover and lived happily.

I would proceed with citing instances of same sex overtones in ancient and medieval India and then focus on the queer representations in the twentieth century Indian English fiction. One of the dominant tropes of same sex love in ancient India is through friendship, often leading to a life of celibacy or the forming of some very intimate relationships. In the ancient Hindu epic, *Mahabharata*, Krishna and Arjuna, frequently referred to as 'the two Krishnas' (Vanita and Kidwai 2000: 3) reflect bonds of friendship which go beyond marriage and procreation. In fact "Krishna clearly states that Arjuna is more important to him than wives, children or kinsmen—there can be many spouses and sons but there is only one Arjuna, without whom he cannot live" (*Ibid.* 5). The Mahabharata, one of the most important epics in Hinduism has numerous other examples of same sex 'attachment' many of which have been discussed by Vanita and Kidwai (2000). However the Krishna and Arjuna friendship remains one of the most important aspects of the epic. A famous conversation in the epic is between Krishna and Arjuna, where Krishna reiterates their inseparability and reveals his divine form to his friend. This collected conversation between the two is the *Bhagvad Gita*, the most widely read Hindu text. When Arjuna's son is still born, Krishna revives him miraculously, "by invoking his own acts of truth and righteousness, foremost amongst which is the perfect love between him and Arjuna" (*Ibid.* 8). Thus, same sex friendship gives life to a new born in this case instead of heterosexual conjugality. At different times and places, primary romantic attachment between men and between women were considered as primary relationship sometimes even over familial ties. As Krishna tells Arjuna:

> Thou art mine and I am thine, while all that is mine is thine also! He that hateth thee hateth me as well, and he that followeth thee followeth me!.... O Partha, thou art from me and I am from thee! 'Besides, puranic stories are replete with accounts of sex change brought through divine intervention. The Hindu deities were multidimensional and fluid in their form and one of their remarkable features was 'their multiplicity and variability'. (*Ibid.* 58)

Thus a deity might appear in any form—male, female, neuter or even in a non-human form. Vishnu, one of the three primary Vedic gods in the Hindu pantheon was also known to take the form of a beautiful woman—Mohini. Shiva, another of the three principle gods, on hearing about his beautiful female form approaches him and asks to see it. Thus, he is aware of the ambiguous nature of Mohini's gender and becomes attracted to her and 'followed her as a lordly elephant would a she elephant' (*Ibid.* 71). The ambiguity in gender here acts as the agency through which same sex desire between the two gods could be realised. Shiva here is not deceived or unaware of Mohini's true gender but knowingly desires and pursues her. Cultural historian, Wendy O'Flaherty remarks that 'the devotees in Shiva see the realisation of all possibilities' (O'Flaherty 1973: 253). This same sex 'encounter' leads to the birth of Ayyappa, who is born of two men. Vanita and Kidwai (2000) says that this legend of the birth was a late medieval addition to the existing story about Shiva and Mohini and it refers to the child as 'ayoni' which refers to non-vaginal sex.

Moving on next to the medieval period, I would like to refer to the Bhakti movement which revolutionized the concept of god and divinity. The gods were no longer worshipped as superior beings but treated as friends and lovers. This led to what J. Rishi says, "the fluidity of gendered structure" (Rishi 2009: 203) between the deity and devotee desire with godly love and also to some extent legitimised same sex. For instance, Surdas and Tulsidas sang praises for a male divine lover.

As Surdas writes:

> These eyes thirst for a vision of Hari (The god Krishna) wanting to see the lotus eyed one
>
> Grieving for him day and night. (Trans by author)

It could easily be read as a poem to a male lover who appears far and distant if these lines are taken out of the Bhakti context. Queer scholar, Ruth Vanita states that male mystic poets visualised themselves as "brides of God". Jagannath Das, a 15th century Oriya poet, was known for his devotion to Shri Chaitanya, a reincarnation of Sri Krishna. In *Jagannath Charitamrita*, Dibakar Das writes, "Overwhelmed with love he held Das in a tight embrace. They stayed in this posture for two days and half." Chaitanya addressed Jagannath as his 'sakhi' (female friend). In Indian narratives, the friend plays a very significant part, as compared to the western ones. Vanita says that, "In miniature paintings, the heroine's female friends are often eroticised. Sometimes they participate in the love play of the hero and heroine, but often they occupy a space of their own in the painting" (Vanita 2005: 92). In this context, O'Flaherty's remark seems revelatory, "[this] celebrate[s] the idea that the universe is boundlessly various and...that all possibilities may exist without excluding each other" (O'Flaherty 1973: 318).

Examples of same sex love representations in ancient and early medieval India is negligible when compared to those found in later medieval period especially those describing love between men during the Perso Arabic invasions in India. In this context, we can refer to Mahmud of Ghazna's relation with his slave, Ayaz and compared his love that of the legendary lovers like Heer and Ranjha, Laila and Majnu. The visibility of homoerotic love affairs was due to the "cosmopolitanism of urban islamic culture", says Saleem Kidwai (Kidwai 2000: 108). In Perso Arabic mystic poetry and in Sufi literature this love is expressed in homoerotic metaphors, however as Kidwai asserts, "many Sufis insisted that only same gender love could transcend sex and therefore not distract the seeker" (Vanita and Kidwai 115). J. Wafer talks about the theme of male-male love in Persian poetry and divides them in three categories-poets who practiced 'shahid-bazi' (Love of boys), poets who used the symbolism of male-male love but prevented acquiring a reputation and thirdly poets who wrote against 'shahid-bazi' (Wafer 1997b: 117). Abru (1733c) and Mir Taqi Mir (1810c) also represented homoeroticism in their poems. "They openly discussed their attraction to males, dwelt on what they found attractive in young males...and heartbreaks" (Vanita and Kidwai, 2000: 119). Whilst poets like Khusro, Abru and Mir frankly talked about the male beloved, others like Hafiz and Attar used the symbolism where the meaning is vague. Attar saw the reflection of God's beauty in the human form. His poems "[oscillate] between the love of a boy and the desire for god" (*Ibid.* 124). Attar too uses the Mahmud and Ayaz romance in his works. Poets such as Jalal-ud-Din-Rumi who was critical of 'shahid-bazi'. He says for example, The Sufi is he who seeks purity, not he who wears a garment of wool, patches it, and commits sodomy (*Ibid.* 126). Rahman says that these poems 'neither celebrate nor denigrate homosexual love...they accept it as a natural outlet for erotic feelings, and are quick to use pseudo mystical arguments against any religious-minded detractor. In short they do not feel stigmatised at all" (Rahman 1990: 18). The Sufi is he who seeks purity, not he who wears a garment of wool, patches it, and commits sodomy (*Ibid.* 126).

With more authors choosing homosexual themes for their work, a same-sex story now no longer remains a taboo for Indian writers. Earlier, novels on same-sex relationships were rare in Indian writing in English. But in the past couple of years, this scenario is undergoing a change. Mayur Patel's novel, 'Vivek and I', is about a teacher who fancies a student in his school. The book was released in December 2010. In July last year, R. Raja Rao, wrote *Hostel Room 131*—a novel tracing a budding love story in the hostel of an engineering college. Incidentally, his novel, *The Boyfriend* (2003) is among the first gay novels written in English in India. Also published last year was Rahul Mehta's *Quarantine*, a collection of short stories. Continuing the trend, this year will see the release of Ghalib Shiraz Dhalla's novel *The Exiles*, about a homosexual man's extra-marital relationship.

Raja Rao's stories constitute a milestone in Indian gay literature. These are candid accounts of men who love men or who are not loved by men. Rao is outspoken about the depradation of Indian gay men experience and his explicit writing denounces the rejection and nonconforming feelings they receive from Indian society. Like Mahesh Dattani, Rao deals with the confines of same sex feelings and always manages to portray a wide range of human experience in a direct unpretentious style. Raja Rao's novel, *The Boyfriend* (2003), is usually considered to be the first book to be fully pivoted around homosexuality. It steered postcolonial fiction towards a new territory where queerness came forth as the central theme. It tells of the romance between Yudi, an upperclass journalist in his 40's and a 19-year-old Dalit boy lover, Milind Mahadik, an office boy. When hired by a modelling agency, Milind disappears from Yudi's life. Distraught at the loss of his boyfriend, Yudi starts spending more time with Gauri, his girlfriend and an upcoming painter who is in love him. Milind returns home when he discovers that his family has arranged his marriage with a girl of their choice. Milind agrees as he never thought of himself as a part of gay culture. After marriage, Milind faces financial restraints and on his wife's advice, calls Yudi for a sexual encounter. Later, it becomes a routine affair, Milind going to Yudi for gaining monetary favours.

The plays in English by Mahesh Dattani, a contemporary Indian playwright deal with the invisible issues of Indian society. With *On a Muggy Night in Mumbai*, Dattani is the first Indian playwright to treat openly homosexual themes of love, partnership and social identity. In an interview, Dattani affirms provocatively: "You can talk about feminism, because in a way that is accepted, but you can't talk about gay issues, because that is not Indian, it doesn't happen here."

Coming to the contemporary scenario of Indian Queer sexuality, as depicted by women writers, the 1996 Deepa Mehta film, *Fire* marks a critical moment. When *Fire* was released in November 1998, it provoked unprecedented conflict. It was condemned by the Right-wing Hindu organizations who considered it to be an assault on "Indian" culture and sensibilities on various levels. The movie was criticized for its depiction of a lesbian relationship between the daughters-in-law of a traditional household, for its choice of the name of India's beloved epic heroine Sita for one of the characters, for its consistent use of the trope of the Hindu epic *Ramayana* for a filmic narrative that valorized female same-sex desire (Deepa Mehta 1996).

In the decades prior to 1998, when the lesbian was not visible in Indian culture, works representing her came from women writers canonized within postcolonial Indian literary studies under the category 'feminist writers' or 'women writers'. The most important examples of these are Urdu writer Ismat Chughtai (1911-91), whose short story *The Quilt* (1941) is a test-case for the stakes in regulating female same-sex desire, something that the attacks against *Fire*, too, illustrated. *The Quilt* became the subject of obscenity charges brought against Chughtai by the colonial British Government in power at the time, for its representation of lesbian desire. The story is the account of a young girl who witnesses the lesbian encounter between a rich Begum and the Begum's servant woman.

The recently deceased Malayalam writer Kamala Das (1934-2009) is the other famous author who represents lesbian desire in her autobiography, *My Story* (1976), and short story *The Sandal Trees* (1988). In the autobiography, Das discusses accounts of female same-sex desire that she witnessed as a girl in a boarding school as well as her own attraction to her female teachers. She also includes a discussion of the intense physical closeness she feels for a female doctor who treated her during an episode of life-threatening illness, an episode that is clearly the basis for her short story years later. For, *The Sandal Trees* is premised on the visit of an unmarried doctor with a married woman, during which both reminisce about their girlhood affair and the doctor attempts to re-kindle it without success. Rosemary George reads Das' contradictory accounts of the verity of the autobiography as the classic evidence of its 'queer' politics for the very instability of the genre suggests, according to George, the instability of heterosexual desire. Ruth Vanita reads the premise of *The Sandal Trees* as establishing the pattern of girlhood affairs that end with the marriage of one or both protagonists in Indian fiction about lesbian desire.

Another autobiographical work that dealt with lesbianism is *Goja: An Autobiographical Myth* (2000) written by Suniti Namjoshi a lesbian feminist, who comes out openly and boldly as a lesbian and considers her defiance of social norms as a counter-attack on gender exploitation. She used autobiography, fantasy and myth in her work. The book is written to two dead women Goja, her childhood friend and Goldie, her grandmother. It is the confession that she could not make in her lifetime that she is making now and one can feel the agony that she experienced as a result of her sexual choice which her heterosexual family saw as wrong and a sin. The book is important as it deals with various issues, how the writer left India because the sexual climate here would have stifled and suppressed and never allowed freedom of choice in sexual behaviour and yet her difficulties in a foreign land were no less as there too she suffered from triple jeopardy being a non-native, a woman and that too a lesbian. She says, "I should like to point out to all the queens and princesses that ever there were that no woman is a first-class human being. She's second-class. And anyway I was a lesbian so presumably, I would have been a third-class human being in any society, wherever it was in the wide world" (Namjoshi 2000: 110).

In Shobha De's *Strange Obsession*, Amrita, a young, budding model encounters Minx, who charms Amrita by her helpful nature. What Minx appears to be and what she exactly is—Amrita is not even remotely aware of it. She is considered as a normal friend by Amrita but what ensues later turns into a nightmare for her. Minx invades every segment of her life and makes things impossible for Amrita. Every moment of Amrita is filled with fear and she practically feels Minx breathing down her neck at any given time of the day or night. So strange is the obsession of Minx for Amrita that when her pursuance to obtain Amrita fails, she fabricates an emotional, projecting her own father as a rapist and villain to gain Amrita's confidence. "Listen...My father...yes...the same man who is so powerful, so respected, so feared...is a beast. A beast of the worst kind. He...He...raped me" (De 1992: 45).

This revelation softens Amrita's heart slightly, but not to the extent that she could accept her love. Minx continues to stalk Amrita and views everyone who wished to help Amrita as an arch rival. When a young chap Rover, shows interest in Amrita, Minx gets him terribly bashed up by the police. Another time she attacks a model who had snatched away a prestigious modelling contract from Amrita. Amrita is filled with abhorrence for Minx when she coolly states how she had 'fixed' the model Lola's face: "Acid baby, acid. Easy to carry. Easy to throw. No hassles. It does the job thoroughly and cleanly. In seconds. Oof! You should've heard her screams" (De 1992: 61). Karan, an ad director also withdraws from Amrita's life when he comes to know of Minx's interest in her and so do many others. A charming editor, Partha, seems to be capable of helping Amrita out of the quicksand pond but Minx makes him meet with a near fatal accident. Minx walks into Amrita's home into Delhi also and by her skillful tactics drives her parents to believe that she is true well-wisher and guardian of Amrita. Eventually Amrita finds herself so terribly entrapped in Minx's web that she feels there is just no escaping from Minx's clutches and the best way was to succumb instead of putting up a fight. Resistance had led her nowhere so she ultimately breaks down, not out of love or concern but out of fear and total helplessness.

In contrast to the other Indian fiction writers who focus on a historical view, Manju Kapur stresses on the complex portrayal of the social and communal unrest. The focus here shifts from a woman's rebellion against society shackled in traditions, torn between duty and desire, to an exploration of the positioning of women in sexual orientation. In the Indian Homophobic socio-cultural context, where any overt expression of sexuality by women is considered as promiscuity, Kapur's novel, *A Married Woman*, explores the twin explosive subjects of sexual intimacy between women and Hindu Muslim confrontation, against a backdrop of respectable middle class Delhi life.

With women as its central theme once again, Kapur raises the question of identity which has been related to the representation of lesbians in literature and culture. Even Shobha De in *Starry Nights* and *Strange Obsession* has extensively dealt with the theme of lesbianism, Deepa Mehta too, in her film *Fire* focused and projected the world of lesbian utopia. However, though the novel approaches this "women-identified experience," it does not specifically address lesbians or present an ideal role model in the protagonist who "could be emulated by the invisible lesbian community in Indian society". The novel should not simply be assessed as a rendition of lesbian relationship. Set at a time of socio-political upheaval, *A Married Woman* is a well-balanced depiction of a country's inner development—its strengths and its failures and anguish of a woman's unrest, which is as complicated as the social and political upheaval going around her." Manju Kapur has beautifully combined love, family values, communal riots, a married woman's life and how she finds love in a person of the same sex. The novel beautifully chronicles the socialist generation of India's post-independence, dealing with self-imposed limitations, socio-economic privations and a yearning for much more. Cast in the rising independence of urban women from the shackles of feminist rhetoric, *A Married Woman* expects the acknowledgement of oppression and the inability of the individual, to effect change in the circumstances, despite the antagonistic forces and expectations of the family and society.

Kapur's preoccupation with displacement of individual and repression is culturally universal. The novels preoccupation with the displacement and repression felt by tradition bound women is evident from the opening of the novel,—"Astha was brought up properly as befits a woman with large supplements of fear" (Kapur 2003: 1). Astha, a young romantic girl drawn to the idea of a love marriage succumbs to the desperation of her perpetually anxious parents, who wish to see her safely married, as they were on the verge of retirement. She rebelliously refuses every suitor, until she meets Hemant whose time at university in the States has turned him into a liberal thinker. Or so she hopes. But as Hemant becomes increasingly involved in his business, Astha finds herself consigned to a traditional female role and discontent slips in. Astha has reached a state of ennui, with her comfortable middle class existence and yearns for more than the quotidian woman's role as a helpmate or a sexual object succumbing to the pressures of society and her family, she never acknowledged her inner desires and aspirations. Astha has little to complain about, and yet she operates as if it is society's greatest crime to limit an individual's passions merely because she is a woman.

Her growing dissatisfaction is played out against a background of Indian political and social unrest. Hit by existential angst, she begins an internal rebellion against the life of repression and anguish. Her convictions are put to the test when she finds not one, but two outlets for her passions. Following the death of a street theatre activist Aijaz in a communal riot in the troubled early nineties, in the wake of the Hindu Muslim clashes over the Babri Masjid in Ayodhya, Astha connects with a social group. She makes a few paintings to be sold in an exhibition sponsored by the Manch and begins to express her creativity through painting, filling her self-imposed loneliness with art. Ironically Astha passes on the same limiting value that her mother-in-law passed on her "thus teaching her daughter how to devalue her work and passing on the tradition from woman to woman". Later in Ayodhya itself, Astha encounters Pipeelika Khan, a woman qualified in sociology and economics and with a background that is Hindu, on her mother's side, South Indian, who works for a Delhi NGO and who turns out to be Aijaz's widow, having boldly married him across the racial divide. A rapport is quickly established between them. The two connect at multiple levels and are drawn to each other. Against all social norms, the friendship between the two women develops into a fully intimate same sex relationship. Astha is enlivened by their romance, to the point that she begins to fantasize of an independent, unfettered existence, together with Pipeelika. She steals time away to be with her lover, until her husband begins to suspect, so that she might have an independent life.

However, due to the generation gap between them, the younger woman Pipeelika realizes the implausibility of any lasting permanent coexistence and finally she leaves for the US to study for a doctorate and Astha is left with nothing but to return emotionally to her marriage to Hemant. Thus, Astha leaps into the fold, unable to take the leap. *A Married Woman* thus explores Astha's longing for a purpose to her life other than being a wife and mother against a vividly realized backdrop of Indian sectarian politics. The author makes Pipeelika leave for the U.S. is a narrative strategy which Patricia Juliana Smith calls, "lesbian panic" (Smith 1995: 572) a strategy which could be traced in the works of Virginia Woolf, Ellen Moers, Elaine Showalter. As Smith remarks—"the condition of lesbian panic have long been inscribed in narratives by and about women" (Smith 1995: 572). The novel therefore, "is not a lesbian text because lesbian sexuality is depoliticalised and reduced to a matter of private preference" (Hoogland 1997: 21). Astha's choice of heterosexual family, marriage and children along with her private preference for lesbian sexuality, makes one wonder if it is a lesbian text. We are also told that even in the most intimate moments that Astha spends with Pipee she cannot help worrying about her kids. We see her straddling between two worlds—the heterosexual world she opts for and the lesbian world which she enjoys but does not acknowledge, her relation with Pipee, was not the outcome of her sexual desire to be with a woman, it was more an incidental happening resulting from her predicament—"like a woman of straw, her inner life dead, with a man who noticed nothing" (Kapur 2003: 287). 'Emotionally starved' and 'throttled', she seeks her jouissance in the lesbian continuum, but the female bonding managed to provide her only a temporary release, not a permanent solution.

Babyji (2005), is a Bildungsroman by U.S. based Indian writer Abha Dawesar, where Dawesar's girl protagonist is in a relationship with a lower-caste woman; heteronormativity is dismantled through lesbian love. Anamika Sharma the protagonist is a young sixteen-year-old teenager who is involved with three women and she enjoys her lesbian relationship in quick succession with all three of different age groups and belonging to a definite social strata. Attack on patriarchal structure of society, male domination and India's rigid social structure are woven into the matrix of this lesbian story.

In Anita Nair's *Ladies Coupe* (2001), Marikolanthu is of a different class, from the other women. She is a maidservant who learns about lesbian love from two foreign mistresses. Every night, I watched Missy K leave her room and walk past me...and go into Missy V's room. In the early hours, she crept back to bed. Why this secrecy, I wondered. If Missy K was afraid to sleep alone, the sensible thing to do would be for them to share a bed. I would have thought nothing of two women sharing a bed. It was the most obvious thing to when men weren't around. For the women to stick together (Nair 2001: 232). Having returned home, she uses the lessons in caresses for her local mistress Sujata, the daughter-in-law of the aristocratic household. The acceptability of women "sticking together" is what Marikolanthu uses to forge her relationship with Sujata, where desire, however intense, remains unspoken. To protect the mistress from her husband's unwanted lovemaking, she selflessly makes love to the man instead, believing all the time that she is doing her mistress a favour by keeping the husband from going off to another woman. It is an act of love on her part which unfortunately alienates her from the women. The reaction of the mistress however after some time is as if she has woken up from a stupor and accuses the protagonist of using black magic on her and making her indulge in unnatural acts. This reaction however is not new and lesbianism is always seen as unnatural and vile. This book by stating the obvious forces us to think about lesbianism as a natural act of love, love as natural and committing as between a man and woman. In Nair's *Ladies Coupe*, although same-sex desire does not ultimately survive the fracturing effect of the discourses of class and caste yet Lesbianism is an illustration of feminine freedom of choice though she remains ignorant, of course, of the actual word.

In Rita Garg's *Precursor of Love*, the Girl, as she is referred to in the entire novel, is a woman who has a series of female partners. Her carefree behaviour, her effervescent attitude, her smile and her confidence—all these qualities make her a very popular girl and it is these qualities that attract Amilya, the protagonist of the novel, to the Girl. The Girl, an exporter by profession has a chance encounter with Amilya at a fair. "Although Amilya has not seen her earlier; even then, something eye—catching is attractive enough about the stranger" (Garg 2006: 1). Another accidental encounter and they both become friends. Amilya was an orphaned lawyer who suffered from loneliness and in the Girl, she looks for a friend. On the contrary, the Girl had been in and out of many lesbian relationships and was nursing the wounds of her last failed relationship when her eyes fall upon Amilya and she thinks that she has found her mate. The desire to come out with her maiden novel makes Amilya get friendly with the Girl as she eyes the Girl as a character for her novel. Her jocularity is her USP and her multi-faceted features make her an ideal literary character in the eyes of Amilya: "The Girl has the typicality of the moon—always changing in form and shape. Nothing can be so effervescent as she. Sometimes, she talks much affectionately but the next moment there is rigour. The talks may be positive now and a total negation next second" (Garg 2006: 14). The Girl enjoys the status of being a 'man' in the relationship and even behaves like one. Though Amilya is senior to her in age yet it is the Girl who seems to have an upper hand in the relationship and Amilya meekly submits to her. Amilya finds herself bound into a strong emotional relationship with the Girl and considers it her first religious binding to keep the Girl jubiliant. Amilya is often torn in a mental conflict whenever the tempest of the Girl's mood swings arises, but the Girl uses her emotional tactics to mellow down Amilya. Tears were her last weapon and if they proved insufficient to move Amilya then other Instruments of emotion were used to victimize her: "If you don't listen to me, I will do something to myself. I would kill myself" (Garg 2006: 36). This was enough to make Amilya follow her like a domestic animal. Initially Amilya befriends the Girl due to her need for a character for her novel but later the seed of emotions gets sown and they become mutually interdependent. Their relationship starts presuming shapes and taking dimensions. The Girl desires consummation but never speaks very openly about it for the fear of losing Amilya. On one occasion when she could not control her emotions and blurts out her desires to see Amilya bedecked in a red saree at the time of their consummation, Amilya is taken aback and the Girl apologizes for the same.

An astonishing feature about their relationship is that the Girl is never vociferous or insistent about anything. She does not put Amilya under any compulsion. On the contrary, Meenakshi Iyengar or Minx as she is called in Shobha De's, *Strange Obsession*, was an emotionally aggressive woman. One could also compare her to a Patient of Obsessive Compulsive Disorder as she shows insane interest in Amrita. Her liking for Amrita cannot be equated with the Girl's liking for Amilya in *Precursor of Love* or that of Pipeelika for Aastha in *A Married Woman*. The other two can be termed as natural, but Minx is paranoid about Amrita. There is nothing natural in her attraction to Amrita as the terror she unleashes for making Amrita hers is spine chilling.

All the three novels studied above have a common thread of lesbianism running through them.

QUEER SEXUALITIES IN R. RAJ RAO'S *THE BOYFRIEND*

> Bombay is a city humming, throbbing with sexual energy. A city of migrant men without women; a city in heat. The womanless rickshaw wallahs, the Bollywood wannabes, the fashion models, and sailors from many countries—all in search of some heat, a hurried furtive fuck in whatever hidden corner the world will permit them. They do it in trains, railway stations, the back of taxis, parks, urinals.
>
> Suketu Mehta, *Maximum City: Bombay Lost and Found*

Over the past several decades our cultural conversations on homosexuality have dramatically changed. It has moved to centre stage in our public discourse with ongoing debates in media, church pulpits, polling booths and courtrooms across the globe. Although the word "queer" has a history of being used as a demeaning or derogatory reference to gay men and lesbians, the term was reclaimed by a group of people who challenged society's sexual and gender norms; gay men, lesbians, transsexuals, transvestites, intersex individuals and anyone else who fell outside traditional heterosexual patterns. For all these people, queerness was to be celebrated challenging the assumption that heterosexuality should set societal standards.

The parameters of homosexuality in the Indian Civil society and in the government have undergone many changes too. Chapter XVI, Section 377 of the Indian Penal Code dating back to 1860, introduced during the British regime in India, criminalised sexual activities "against the order of nature", arguably including homosexual acts. On 2 July 2009, the Delhi High Court delivered a judgement in favour of Naz Foundation, an organisation that works for same-sex equality, declaring that the application of Section 377 of the Indian Penal Code that penalised consensual sex among adults was unconstitutional. However, that judgement was overturned by the Supreme Court of India on 12 December 2013, with the Court holding that amending or repealing Section 377 should be a matter left to Parliament, not the judiciary.

R. Raj Rao's *The Boyfriend* (2003) examines the controversial projection of homosexuality as a significant distinction for men who experience same-sex desire in 1992 Bombay. In Rao's novel, individuals negotiate same-sex desires within a socio-political construct controlled by the heteronormative culture of Bombay in the 1990s. The sexualities of the gay protagonists endangers this construct of culture because they do not comply to the reproductive model of opposite-sex desire.

"For a city that has more homosexuals than London and Paris put together, Mumbai's gay subculture has been a well-kept secret. R. Raj Rao's *The Boyfriend*, however, is telling it all. Yudi, a freelance journalist in Nalla Sopara and an out gay man finds in his 40s that sex with strangers just doesn't cut it for him any more," remarked Sehgal (indiatoday.intoday.in›...› Books› June 2, 2003).

She gives a very graphic decription, "Following Yudi through editor's offices, art openings, filthy toilets and Testosterone, the one gay bar in the city, *The Boyfriend* pictures an unsentimental Mumbai—a crazy, cruel, layered and labyrinthine city, both physically and psychologically, full of cultural chaos and class conflict, where people stumble through their lives, making a buck, pushing their luck, looking for love in all the wrong places.

R. Raj Rao is a writer, academic and queer activist based in Pune, India; *The Boyfriend*, published in 2003, is an important landmark in queer-themed fiction coming out of South Asia. Dubbed as a 'cult classic' by readers and scholars alike Rao's novel, *The Boyfriend* presents Raj Rao's projection of an 'essentialist, sacrosanct homosexuality' which unites men who love and have sex with men due to their shared humiliation. Commenting on Rao's academic and creative writing on queer themes, Andrew Grossman calls him a "radical utopian" (2001: 299). In this context, Rao's analysis in the introduction to Whistling in the Dark of Foucault's oft-cited remark on the normalisation of homosexuality seems rather poignant: The French philosopher Foucault says: "One day the question, 'Are you a homosexual?' will be as natural as the question, 'Are you a bachelor?'"

"A speechless Yudi welcomed his Milya with open arms. He wasn't at all bitter about the manner in which Milya had dumped him. He was too old for self-respect, and too much in love. Tears flowed down his cheeks. His heart was full of gratitude and joy, so that when his prodigal lover complained about how long he had walked, Yudi sat the boy down and knelt before him to massage his chapped and weary feet. From the far end of the room, two pairs of eyes watched Yudi risk rebirth as a shit-worm by touching the feet of a Bhangi. The eyes belonged to Gauri" (Rao 2003: 226-27).

The scene from Raj Rao's novel *The Boyfriend* shows Yudi Pandava, the well-educated and moneyed Brahmin protagonist, meeting his impoverished Dalit lover, Milind Mahadik, after a long parting. The melodramatic depiction of Yudi's "speechless" reaction of "joy" and "tears" critiques Yudi's subservience, ascertained through the eyes of the apparently liberal though basically conservative Gauri.

The Boyfriend presents Yudi's Brahmanism as one of the inevitable components of identity which co-occurs and overlaps with his wilful Westernised homosexual bearings and precludes its fitting exemplification. Apart from depicting the Brahmin/Dalit fissure, Rao demarcates Yudi and Milind by asserting that the former self-identifies as "radically gay", while the latter falls below the scope of Anglophone identity politics (193). Even when the two men are sexually or romantically together, they are separated by the ideological differences ingrained in their class and caste, a leitmotif which contributes to Rao's delineation of Yudi's more general social estrangement.

The novel describes the life of Yudi, a forty-something self-proclaimed gay and who is emphatically middle-class and atheist, qualities which are seen to complement his work as a journalist. Capitalising on the opportunities presented by male homosocial spaces in 1990s Bombay, he enjoys a licentious lifestyle and frequently has sex in public locations.

Space plays a pivotal role in *The Boyfriend*, in which the majority of chapter titles refers to spaces/places where important events occur: "Testosterone," "Mate House," "Shravanabelagola," "Chaitya Bhoomi," and "A.K. Modelling Agency". Throughout the novel, the sense of movement is present—sometimes hectic, sometimes indolent, sometimes mediated (railway transportation). The novel reveals an endless meandering in and out of different spaces that Yudi—the gay journalist who is the central character in the novel—inhabits or visits or travels through. This meandering is essentially urban in nature: the Bombay landscape spreads out before Yudi as he moves around on an erotic quest—he "haunts" the city streets and its local trains. Yudi and Milind's courtship occurs in the dark corners of Café Volga and amidst the psychedelic lights of the gay nightclub Testosterone, their brief time as a couple is portrayed within the confines of Yudi's bachelor apartment (affectionately and flippantly dubbed Mate House), and their honeymoon happens in Shravanabelagola (a tourist destination in the neighbouring state of Karnataka).

As a gay man in Bombay, Yudi is aware of the spaces in which he can seek out this sexual satisfaction. The first queer space that Rao reveals is the men's bathroom at Churchgate Station. Situated at the end of the train's run through Bombay, men accumulate to have casual and anonymous sex. Yudi's depiction of the place is both vulgar and worshipful as if it were a sanctified space:

> The stinking places were always humming with erotic activity. Orgies in the dark, amidst piss and shit. The foul smell, somehow, made the sex more enjoyable. Having spent so much of his life in these loos Yudi had come to the conclusion that there was indeed something sensual about filth. If the toilets were clean, scrubbed with phenyl, patrons wouldn't achieve orgasm. (28)

Yudi goes out of the toilets with a sense of belonging to something outside of the heteronormative world:

> This was the most urgent of factors that drove him to Churchgate. The gents' toilet at Churchgate provided a twenty-four-hour supply of men; the amount of semen that went down the urine bowls was enough to start a sperm bank. (2)

The priority of sexual contact in Yudi's life secludes him from heteronormative social constructs: his mother is confined to

Sunday visits and "in his opinion that was more than enough," while his employer and co-workers "knew that he was gay; and they knew that he knew that they knew," but such a description evokes a sense of social distance allowing for the possibility "that in their heart of hearts, they thought he was weird" (28). Therefore, the heterosexuals in Yudi's life are tangential, with little more than acquaintance and obligatory congenial interaction without a sense that they understand Yudi personally. Even his friend Gauri uses him for her own purposes: "There was no objective correlative between Gauri's knowledge of Yudi's sexual orientation, and her behaviour. She continued to think of him as a possible husband. In his private lingo, she was the 'Backbay Reclamation' kind. She assumed that all men were naturally attracted to women. If something about their sex life had gone awry, there was no reason why they couldn't be reclaimed, reformed" (52). Gauri tries to modify Yudi, into a heteronormative space by constructing a changing sensitivity of his carnal desires.

Yudi can only escape these pressures to perform heterosexuality within the sacred spaces of queer sexual desire that he has created for himself for casual sexual encounters. The spaces in which Yudi and Milind can experience same-sex intimacy are on the move throughout the book. The most important of these spaces is the train. Yudi meets and falls in love with a much younger Dalit man, Milind, with whom he has a distinctive and mutually calculating relationship. Eventually, Milind's family marry him off to a woman of his own caste, and he shears off his contact with Yudi. At the end of the novel, Milind, impoverished in his new marriage, returns to Yudi to restart their relationship, unashamedly demanding his "pocket money (arrears plus interest)" (230). Thus, the novel emerges as a cynical exposé of the power struggles created by the imbrications of a gay or homosexual identity and other longer-standing identifications in India. When Yudi first meets Milind (at this stage going by the false name of Kishore) in Churchgate Station, Rao emphasizes the great difference between them. Yudi is a "prolific freelancer" who is said to earn "at least thirty grand a month"; while he is over forty and "beginning to grey at the temples", Milind is "a guy in his late teens, twenty at most" (3). Their first sexual contact is rather estranging:

> He brought his left hand towards the young man's crotch.... No sooner was he touched there, than the boy started in fear. How could anyone be so shameless! He gasped silently. Yudi, ignorant of the boy's confusion, drew closer. The odour of sweat from the young working-class body made his head spin, but then he noticed the lad's feet. The fellow was wearing slippers. The feet were as shapeless as a leper's, like the feet of most men who came to Churchgate. The uncut toenails were pallid. There were cracks on the soles, especially visible around the heels. Yuk, Yudi burped. The boy abruptly moved away. (6-7)

Yudi and Milind's conflicting approaches are epitomised in the latter's "silent gasp", a harbinger of the men's persistent inability to express their innermost feelings. Despite the delicate exchange of prospects here, there is no real connection, obstructed as it is by disparity in age, class, caste and sexual identity. Yudi externalizes the "working-class" body in his swaying between fatalism and hatred, and an inescapable sense of isolation is created by his synecdochic weakening of Milind into de segregated physical traits: "the odour of sweat", "a pair of slippers" and "uncut toenails". Rao ultimately develops the men's physical differences into essential socio-economic disparities. Milind demands that Yudi lives in a "posh area" and asks him what language he speaks at home. Yudi replies, "English", "quickly" adding "and Hindi" (9) in a half-hearted attempt to downplay the privilege of the Anglophone classes. Milind cannot understand Yudi's 'upper-class' English and Yudi is unable to follow Milind's 'working-class' Marathi, a sociolinguistic barrier which is also responsible for their varying sexual and gender self-identifications.

Before their first sexual encounter, Milind tries to define Yudi's religion, hoping that he is not a "Mohammedan" because "They're unclean". The latter remains silent as "he had no desire to educate the boy about the ills of bigotry" (9), but his assumption that Milind will blackmail him after sex is equally partisan, recalling his antagonistic reactions of attraction and repulsion in Churchgate. Although Yudi seeks such subaltern men out as lovers, his ambivalence is bound up with the ineffaceable sense of superiority of the higher classes. Rao adopts a comparable strategy of inversion regarding Milind's Dalit and Yudi's Brahmin status; when Milind warns him that he is an untouchable, Yudi responds:

> "May I kiss you on the mouth?"... It was his way of demonstrating that he cared two fucks if Milind was a Brahman or a Bhangi, whose ancestors cleaned the shit of others....
>
> The more down-and-out Milind was, the more they would click. Outcastes, after all, can only expect to be friends with outcastes. (74)

Yudi's intended alliteration of "Brahman" and "Bhangi" appears to break down the divide between the two, an action reinforced by his hyperbolic vision of his own debasement as an "outcaste". We recall Rao's contention for the equality of the homosexual and the coolie/peon in "Underground", but Yudi's choice to live as openly gay is not comparable to the determinism of Milind's caste inheritance. In both cases their alleged friendship is read aloud by the upper middle class Brahmin, and degrees of disparagement go uncredited; an untouchable who apparently loves and has sex with men definitely has less social currency than his upper-caste gay counterpart. Rao does not allow Yudi's idealistic vision to go unhampered, instead revealing it as illogical and contradictory. To confirm whether or not Yudi is really bothered by his caste, Milind advises him to eat several wafers which he has half eaten, and Yudi reacts angrily:

> "Homos are no different from Bhangis. Both are Untouchables. So why should I have a problem with eating your jootha?"
>
> "But you are a Brahman, aren't you?"
>
> "No, I am a homosexual. Gay by caste. Gay by religion."
>
> "I don't understand what you are saying."
>
> "What I am saying is that homosexuals have no caste or religion. They have only their homosexuality."

> "How can that be?"
>
> "That's how it is. Straight people are Brahmans, gays Shudras. So you see, both you and I are Shudras. That's why we are best friends."

Milind seems to understand that Yudi was right though he was in no position, however, to understand the intricacies of the argument (81-82). However much he protests, Yudi cannot escape what Mulk Raj Anand (2005) in his 1935 novel Untouchable calls "six thousand years of racial and class superiority" (16): the homosexual relationship can never be disentangled from the complex networks of class, caste, religion, and other expressions and determinants of power. Observing the gigantic statue of the Jain saint Gomateshwara in the city of Shravanabelagola, Yudi is about to make an inflammatory remark on the size of its genitals, and the two men quarrel again:

> "Shut up!" Milind snapped. "Have some respect for a sacred place. You're so educated, yet you talk such rubbish!"
>
> "Let me put it this way," said Yudi, not accustomed to being snubbed. "I talk rubbish because I'm educated. At least I have something to say. You illiterates are slaves. You only say what people allow you to!" (126)

The Boyfriend arduously shows that Yudi and Milind are separated by class, caste, age, language, education and religion, and, in a society where such formulations constantly militate against fulfilling relationships, even gay idealism cannot appear uncoloured by social conditioning. Rao's position reminds us of Dennis Altman (2001), who speaks about the 'developing world':

> The romantic myth of homosexual identity cutting across class, race, and so on doesn't work in practice any more than it does in the West. The experience of sexuality in everyday life is shaped by such variables as the gap between city and country; ethnic and religious differences; and hierarchies of health, education, and age. The idea of a gay or lesbian/gay community assumes that such differences can be subordinated to an overarching sense of sexual identity, a myth that is barely sustainable in comparatively rich and affluent societies. (34)

Yudi connects this sex act with being homosexual (or gay), constructing an identity that crosses boundaries of caste and seeks queer spaces in a community defined by its common rejection of heteronormative constructs of sexuality. This means that queer spaces for Yudi are available to a variety of same-sex identities including drag queens, MSMs, hijras, and koti. However, Milind defines himself primarily by his caste as a Bhangi (74) and his traditional religion as a follower of Gautama Buddha (74), viewing his sexual desire for men as secondary to the heteronormative spaces in which his identity is defined by his family, religion, and caste. Milind finds himself in conflict with this heteronormative self-construction as he begins to explore same-sex desire. He combines sexual roles with views of masculinity and restricting his experiences to those in which he can visualise himself as manly. What is evident by Yudi's and Milind's differences in self-identification is that social perceptions of the self—such as gay, straight, active, passive, man, and woman are constructed signifiers without an essentialist signified to represent.

Yudi has a quiet understanding with his mother: "She knew why her son was a bachelor, but it wasn't something she could bring herself to talk about, even in her nightmares" (193); still, she refuses to believe that he will never fulfill her expectations of marriage and children. Gauri gives his mother a false hope that she will help him lead the expected life of an adult male: "her presence in the flat made his mom happy. A ray of hope arises in her heart: "could it be that her son was turning normal?" (193). Because they live in silence, Yudi's sexuality is not real or material. Therefore, in his mother's eyes, Yudi's single lifestyle perpetuates his childhood. Meanwhile, Milind avoids his family. He does not go home because he does not want them to be aware of his relationship with Yudi or his life as a prostitute with the A.K. Modelling Agency. When Yudi invades this family space in a desperate search for the boy, Milind is horrified: "he had become the laughing stock of his family. See how the sight of Yudi amused his mother and brother! Look at the way his parents compared the chhakka to macho friends like Pramod and David, and found him wanting! [...]. They must have suspected there was something odd about the whole thing" (207). His family begin to see the nature of their relationship and in turn they encourage Yudi's presence with an invitation to Milind's brother's wedding. Because he is of a higher caste, they see Yudi's sexual interests as a means of earning an income—so long as Milind still marries and fulfills his heteronormative expectations. Milind's wife Leela encourages the prostitution of her own husband, sending Milind off to beg for money not fully comprehending the sexual exchange this will entail:

> Milya had a friend who earned five thousand rupees for every article he sent to the *Times of India*. If that was the case he must be rich, filthy rich. Of course, she did not think the man would be a Krishna to her family—for gods were gods and men were men—but where was the harm in asking for help anyway? She was not to know that unlike Krishna and Sudama, her husband and the journalist—corrupt mortals, after all—were both more and much less than friends. (223)

In the end, we find Yudi back on the cruising scene, disillusioned by Milind's submission to the heterosexual institution of marriage, but aware of the fact that this changing shades of identities is the only form of existence available to him.

Bombay is a city of contradictions: at once the place which nurtures queer subcultures, a city that serves as a center stage for queer activism. For men like Rao's Yudi, the transience of flanerie—made possible by the co-existence and mainstream and alternative spaces in the urban landscape of Bombay—is the only way to perform their queer identity.

Works Cited

Bhardwaj, Kajal "Reforming Macaulay". Narrain and Elridge eds. *The Right that Dares to Speak its Name: Discriminating Sexual Orientation and Gender Identity in India*. Bangalore. Alternative Law Forum, 2009.

Burton, Antoinette. *Dwelling in the Archive: Women Writing House, Home, and History in Late Colonial India*. New York: Oxford University Press, 2003.

Chughtai, Ismat. *The Quilt*. 1941. *Ismat Chughtai: The Quilt and Other Stories*. Ed. and transl. Tahira Naqvi and Syeda S. Hameed. New Delhi: Kali for Women, 1996: 5-12.

Das Kamala. *The Sandal Trees*. 1988. *The Sandal Trees and Other Stories*. Transl. V.C. Harris and C.K. Mohamed Ummer. Hyderabad: Dish, 1995: 1-26.

Das, Kamala. *My Story*. Jullundur: Sterling, 1976.

Dawesar, Abha. *Babyji*. New York: Anchor, 2005.

De, Shobha. *Strange Obsession*, New Delhi: Penguin India, 1992.

Eldeman, Lee (1995). "Queer Thory: Unstating Desire", *GLQ: A Journal of Lesbian and Gay Studies* 2, 4: 343-46.

Foucault, M. (1996). *History and Homosexuality* (L. Hochroth and J. Johnston, Trans.). In S. Lotringer (Ed.), Foucault Live (Interviews, 1961-84). New York: Semiotext(e).

Garg, Rita. *Precursor of Love*. New Delhi: Vishwabharti Publications, 2006.

Gay, Ruling. "Now we're really in the 21st century," *The Times of India*, 3 July, 2009. 8 Sept., 2010.

Grossman, A. (Ed.) (2001). *Queer Asian Cinema: Shadows in the Shade*. New York: Harrington Park Press.

Halperin, David (1995). *Saint Foucault: Towards a Gay Hagiography*. New York: Oxford University Press.

Hoogland, Renee C. *Lesbian Configuration*. New York: Columbia University Press, 1997, 21.

Kapur, Manju: *A Married Woman*. London: Faber and Faber, 2003.

Mehta, Deepa, dir. *Fire*. Delhi: Kaleidoscope Entertainment, 1996.

Mehta, Suketu. *Maximum City: Bombay Lost and Found*. New York: Vintage Books, 2005. Print.

Merchant, Hoshang (ed.). *Yaarana—Gay Writings from India*. New Delhi, Penguin India, 1999.

Nair, Anita. *Ladies Coupe*. New Delhi: Penguin, 2001. Print.

Namjoshi, Suniti. *Goja: An Autobiographical Myth*. Melbourne: Spinifex, 2000.

Narrain Arvind and Marcus Elridge, eds. *The Right that Dares to Speak its Name: Discriminating Sexual Orientation and Gender Identity in India*. Bangalore. Alternative Law Forum, 2009.

Narrain, Arvind. "Rethinking Citizenship: A Queer Journey", *Indian Journal of Gender Studies*, 14:1 (2007): 61-71. Print.

Narrain, Arvind and Gautam Bhan, ed. *Because I Have a Voice: Queer Politics in India*. New Delhi: Yoda Press, 2006.

O'Flaherty, W. (1973). *Siva: The Erotic Ascetic*. Oxford: Oxford University Press Sociological Perez, R.M. (2001), "Portuguese Orientalism: Some Problems on Classification," in *The Portuguese and the Socio-cultural Changes in India* 1500-1800. Tellicherry: Institute for Research on Social Sciences and Humanities, Meshar, 7-25.

Rahman, T. (1990). "Boy Love in the Urdu Ghazal," *Annual of Urdu Studies* (7), 1-20.

Ramanujan, A.K. *A Flowering Tree—and Other Oral Tales from India.* New Delhi: Penguin India, 1997: 142.

Rao, R. Raj. *The Boyfriend.* New Delhi: Penguin, 2003. Print.

Rao, R. Raj (2009). Introduction. In R. Rao and D. Sharma (Eds.), *Whistling in the Dark: Twenty-One Queer Interviews.* New Delhi: Stand, 2008: ix-xxxiii. Print.

——. (2003). *The Boyfriend.* New Delhi: Penguin.

Rishi, J. (2009). "Same Sex Love in India: A Literary History Review", *Rupkatha Journal on Interdisciplinary Studies in Humanities*, 1(2): 201-04.

Smith, Patricia Juliana. "*And I wondered if she might kiss me": Lesbian, panic as narrative strategy in British women's fiction in Modern Fiction Studies.* Vol. 41: 3-4, Fall-Winter 1995.

Vanita, R. (2005). *Gandhi's Tiger and Sita's Smile: Essays on Gender, Sexuality and Culture.* New Delhi: Yoda Press.

Vanita, R. and Kidwai S. (2000). *Same Sex Love in India: Readings from Literature and History.* New Delhi: Macmillan.

Wafer, J. (1997a). "Muhammad and Male Homosexuality," Stephen O. Murray and Will Roscoe (ed.), *Islamic Homosexualities.* New York: New York University Press.

Wafer, J. (1997b). "Vision and Passion: The Symbolism of Male Love in Islamic Mystical Literature," Stephen Murray and Will Roscoe (ed.) *Islamic Homosexualities*, New York: New York University Press, 107-31.

Internet source

indiatoday.intoday.in... Books, June 2, 2003.

Index